THE ESSENTIAL LENIN

THE ESSENTIAL LENIN

EDITED BY ERNST FISCHER
IN COLLABORATION WITH FRANZ MAREK

TRANSLATED BY ANNA BOSTOCK

HERDER AND HERDER

1972
HERDER AND HERDER NEW YORK
232 Madison Avenue, New York 10016

Original edition: *Was Lenin wirklich sagte,*
Vienna, Verlag Fritz Molden, 1969.

Library of Congress Catalog Card Number: 73–127871
First published in London in 1972 by The Penguin Press
under the title *Lenin in His Own Words.*
Translation copyright © 1972 by Anna Bostock
Printed in the United States

CONTENTS

TRANSLATOR'S NOTE

The 44 volumes of Lenin's complete works were
published in 1960 by the Foreign Languages
Publishing House in Moscow and distributed in
Britain by Lawrence and Wishart. A considerable
number of translators and editors collaborated in
making this edition available; some were English,
some American, some Russian; different volumes
had different editors. As a result, the standard of
translation is somewhat uneven. But this edition is
the only one available to the British public, and I
therefore had no choice but to use it throughout,
not only for direct quotations but also for the
innumerable concealed quotations contained in
Franz Marek's and Ernst Fischer's text. Whenever
a conflict arose between elegance of style and
complete authenticity, I felt bound to opt for the
latter. Only on one or two occasions where the
English text seemed either incorrect or excessively
unclear have I ventured, in a footnote, to suggest an
alternative reading.

A.B.

BIOGRAPHICAL DATA

1870   22 April: Vladimir Ilyich Ulyanov born at Simbirsk
        (now Ulyanovsk).

1887   20 May: Lenin's eldest brother, A. I. Ulyanov,
        executed for taking part in an attempt on the life of
        Alexander III.
        22 June: Lenin graduates from the gymnasium
        (grammar school), receiving a gold medal.
        August: Lenin enters the University of Kazan. First
        contacts with revolutionary student groups.
        19 December: expelled from Kazan, placed under
        police surveillance.

1888   October: returns to Kazan. First contact with
        Marxist groups.

1889   Moves to Samara.

1890   Translates *The Communist Manifesto*.

1891   As an external student, passes examinations at the
        faculty of law of St Petersburg University.

1893   Reads his first Marxist studies aloud to like-minded
        friends in St Petersburg. First contact with workers.

1894   Lenin assumes the leadership of the Social-Democrats
        of St Petersburg and writes his first major work:

What the 'Friends of the People' Are and How They Fight the Social-Democrats, published legally in several editions.

1895　May: first voyage abroad. In Switzerland Lenin establishes contact with Plekhanov's 'Emancipation of Labour' group. Visits Paris and Berlin.
Autumn: he founds the 'League of Struggle for the Emancipation of the Working Class' in St Petersburg. Leaflets, brochures.
21 December: Lenin is arrested.

1897　10 February: Lenin is sentenced to three years' exile in Siberia. Articles, reviews, translations. He works on his exhaustive study *The Development of Capitalism in Russia*, which he completes in 1899. The work is published legally under the signature 'Vladimir Ilyin'.

1898　Together with N. K. Krupskaya, whom he marries on 22 July, Lenin translates Vol. I of *Industrial Democracy* by Sidney and Beatrice Webb. Publication of Kautsky's *Bernstein and the Social-Democratic Programme*.

1900　10 February: exile ends.
July: Lenin goes abroad.
December: the first issue of *Iskra* is published in Munich.

1902　*What Is To Be Done?* is published in Stuttgart.

1903　Lenin moves to Paris and works among Russian exiles there.
End of April: transfers *Iskra* to Geneva.
30 July – 23 August: Second Congress of the Russian Social-Democratic Labour Party, founded in 1898. The Congress opens in Brussels and is later transferred to London.
1 November: Lenin leaves the editorial board of *Iskra*, on which the Mensheviks have the majority.

1904   19 May: *One Step Forward, Two Steps Back* published in Geneva.

1905   4 January: Lenin's new paper (*Vperyod*) is published in Geneva.
9 January: beginning of revolutionary developments in Russia.

25 April to May: Third Congress of R.S.D.L.P. held under Lenin's chairmanship and without the participation of the Mensheviks.
June – July: *Two Tactics of Social-Democracy in the Democratic Revolution.*
End of October: Lenin travels to Russia.

1906   Fourth (Unity) Congress of the R.S.D.L.P. held in Stockholm with the participation of both factions.

1907   13 May – 1 June: Fifth Party Congress in London.
8 July: Lenin becomes the representative of the Russian Social-Democrats on the International Socialist Bureau.
9 July: *Against Boycott.*
18–23 August: participates in the Stuttgart Congress of the Socialist International.
25 December: beginning of Lenin's second period of emigration.

1908   Writes *Materialism and Empirio-Criticism*, which is published in Moscow in May. Moves from Switzerland to Paris.

1910   Visits Gorky in Capri.
28 August – 3 September: takes part in the Copenhagen Congress of the Socialist International.

1911   End of August: organizes a Party school at Longjumeau near Paris.

1912   18–30 June: the Bolsheviks form a party of their own in Prague. Lenin moves to Cracow to exercise closer editorial control over the new Party paper, *Pravda.*

1913 31 May: *Backward Europe and Advanced Asia* appears in *Pravda*.

July: *Pravda* is banned. Substitute newspapers are published.

1914 January: meeting held in Cracow to discuss the work of the Bolshevik group in the Russian parliament. 8 August: following the outbreak of war, Lenin is arrested by the Austrian authorities. Moves to neutral Switzerland. Essays and brochures on the war, the collapse of the International and related subjects.

1915 August: *On the Slogan for a United States of Europe*. 2–4 September: takes part in the anti-war Zimmerwald Conference, where he organizes the left wing.

1916 Completes his book *Imperialism, the Highest Stage of Capitalism*.

1917 10 March (24 February old style): beginning of revolution in Russia.

20 March: Lenin begins *Letters from Afar*.

9 April: Lenin and Krupskaya leave for Russia.

16 April: arrival at the Finland Station in St Petersburg.

17 April: 'April Theses' on the tasks of the revolution.

22 April: the article *The Dual Power* is published in *Pravda*.

4 July: the July demonstration. Lenin goes into hiding.

8–16 August: Sixth Party Congress of the Bolsheviks held in Lenin's absence.

4 September: Lenin moves to Finland.

August – September: he writes *State and Revolution*. September: *The Impending Catastrophe and How To Combat It, On Compromises, Can the Bolsheviks Retain State Power?, Marxism and Insurrection*, etc.

20 October: return to Petrograd (St Petersburg).

7 November (25 October old style): beginning of armed insurrection. Lenin speaks at a meeting of the Petrograd Soviet.

8 November: he drafts the decrees on peace and land and the decision to form the workers' and peasants' government. Addresses the evening meeting of the All-Russia Congress of Soviets, which elects him Chairman of the Council of People's Commissars.

12 November: broadcast 'To All'.

1918   10 February: telegram to the Russian delegation at the peace conference of Brest-Litovsk demanding the immediate signing of a peace treaty with Germany.

21 February: *The Revolutionary Phrase.*

15 March: Extraordinary Congress of Soviets approves Lenin's stand on the signing of a peace treaty.

28 April: *The Immediate Tasks of the Soviet Government.*

30 August: Lenin is shot and gravely wounded by the Socialist-Revolutionary Fanny Kaplan.

10 November: he completes *The Proletarian Revolution and the Renegade Kautsky.*

1919   2–6 March: Foundation Congress of the Communist International.

28 June: Lenin completes *A Great Beginning.*

30 October: *Economics and Politics in the Era of the Dictatorship of the Proletariat.*

1920   27 April: Lenin completes *'Left-Wing' Communism – an Infantile Disorder.*

19 July – 7 August: Second Congress of the Communist International.

30 December: speech on trade unions.

1921   25 January: Lenin completes the brochure *Once Again on the Trade Unions, the Current Situation and the Mistakes of Trotsky and Bukharin.*

8–16 March: Tenth Congress of the Russian Communist Party (Bolsheviks). Suppression of the Kronstadt rising.

21 April: Lenin completes the brochure *On the Tax in Kind*.

22 June – 12 July: Third Congress of the Communist International.

6 December: Lenin asks Gorky to appeal to G. B. Shaw and H. G. Wells to take part in organizing aid for the famine-stricken in Russia.

1922   End of February: *Notes of a Publicist. On Ascending a High Mountain.*

2 May: *On the Tenth Anniversary of* Pravda.

26 May: beginning of serious illness.

1923   4–6 January: *On Co-operation.*

16–17 January: *Our Revolution.*

2–9 February: *Better Fewer, But Better.*

1924   21 January: death of Lenin.

INTRODUCTION

This book is an attempt by the authors of *Marx in His Own Words*, once more in the space of barely two hundred pages, to present *Lenin in His Own Words*. This time the task is a good deal more difficult. Despite his leading role in the International Working Men's Association, Marx was first and foremost a theoretician; Lenin, despite his theoretical works, was first and foremost the strategist and tactician of revolution.

Marx described the first volume of *Capital* as the most terrible projectile ever hurled at the head of the bourgeoisie. Lenin broke off the manuscript of *State and Revolution* with the following words:

This pamphlet was written in August and September 1917. I had already drawn up the plan for the next, the seventh, chapter, 'The Experience of the Russian Revolutions of 1905 and 1917'. Apart from the title, however, I had no time to write a single line of the chapter; I was 'interrupted' by a political crisis – the eve of the October Revolution of 1917. Such an 'interruption' can only be welcomed; but the writing of the second part of the pamphlet ('The Experience of the Russian Revolutions of 1905 and 1917') will probably have to be put off for a long time. It is more pleasant and useful to go through the 'experience of the revolution' than to write about it.

The Author[1]

Petrograd
November 30, 1917

The seventh chapter was never written: it was dictated to
reality, the contradictory, obdurate reality of revolution which
frustrated many plans, overthrew many notions and corrected
many theories in the light of practice. We see therefore that the
life's work which Marx left behind him is more unified, more
complete, more readily surveyed – for all its prolixity – than
the unfinished life's work of the man who paved the way for
the greatest revolution in history, led it to victory, and left it
behind as a colossal rump: a life's work filled to overbrimming
with extreme situations, harsh antitheses and unexpected
shifts of direction.

The authors (Franz Marek as writer, Ernst Fischer as
adviser and collaborator) were therefore faced with problems
which they see no reason to conceal from their readers. Should
they describe and interpret the events to which Lenin reacted –
theoretically, strategically and tactically – and which he
moulded, partly at least, with his own mind and will? Should
they undertake a critique of Lenin's theories and of his strategic
and tactical decisions, comparing them with other Marxist
theories and attitudes? Or should they, for the most part, let
Lenin speak for himself and offer only such comments as are
essential for an understanding of his words? They opted for the
third method and decided to organize the book under major
headings corresponding to specific sets of problems, selecting
characteristic quotations to illustrate each one. Max Weber
said that selection is in itself a form of value judgement. That
is certainly true of this book.

The Lenin whom our selection is intended to reveal is not
the canonized Lenin, not a saint and Father of the Church, but
a revolutionary leader and thinker, a man with all the contradictions of a man.

When Stalin first attended a meeting of delegates which was
to be addressed by Lenin, he asked when Lenin would be
coming. 'He's over there,' he was told; and he saw an in no

way conspicuous person in the middle of a group of comrades, talking, listening and responding with friendly animation. Stalin was astounded. He had imagined that everyone would sit still and wait for Lenin to speak. Then, suddenly, complete silence fell upon the gathering: the leader, until that moment invisible, mounted the platform.

Mingling with the others, friendly, animated, at ease, incapable of striking a pose or of deliberately putting a distance between himself and his comrades: such was the 'private' Lenin. It is true that all 'private' things were reduced to a minimum, allowed to exist only in the margin of his life. Yet this margin is not irrelevant when we consider such facts as Lenin's reluctance to listen to Beethoven's music because it moved him to tears when he felt he ought to be hard, or the personal help he gave, without the Central Committee's knowledge, to Martov, his political opponent, while attacking him ruthlessly in public. The friendly, helpful, sensitive, unassuming Lenin existed; but the essential Lenin was the man totally absorbed by his cause, devoured by it, identified with it.

In 1887 the Tsar's hangmen executed the eldest brother of Vladimir Ilyich Ulyanov, who was then seventeen years old. A place fell vacant: Lenin stepped into it. From that moment on, his life was *representative* in the deepest sense of the word. It was not so much that he represented, or replaced, his brother; rather, he became the blood-witness of his brother's cause – the cause of revolution against the 'realm of darkness', as Dobrolyubov had called tsarist rule, revolution for the sake of a Russia no longer barbarian but democratic and socialist. Completely at one with this cause, Lenin was incomparably more than its executor: he was at the same time its inspiration, not merely the representative of historical tendencies, but an active force in determining them, influencing their course and accelerating the speed of their development. The cause he embraced was not something already given, formed and complete; its state was like that of molten, incandescent metal which needed a master of the craft to mould it.

Lenin was a volcano of revolutionary passion. A few short film strips in which Lenin the orator has been preserved for posterity reveal this passion, this dynamism and vitality. With every gesture he kneads, shapes, tears apart the words he uses, he throws his whole body into every sentence he speaks, he hurls himself into the mass of people whom he is determined to convince and win over. He wants everyone to understand him, educated Marxists and illiterate peasants alike; he emphasizes, exaggerates, repeats – and suddenly, in the midst of a passage of didactic political agitation, he produces a metaphor of great poetic intensity, like that 'on ascending a high mountain' which Brecht so much admired. Tireless as he was, and capable of making half a dozen speeches or writing half a dozen articles in a single day, he was not afraid of repeating himself: on the contrary, he would say the same thing a hundred times over until it not only stuck to the surface but was absorbed into the very flesh and blood of living men. Many of the essays, proclamations and pamphlets Lenin wrote read like the spoken word. The adjectives succeed one another in a tumbling flood – a single one will not do, he must find a stronger one and then a stronger one yet, there have to be three adjectives at least, sometimes five or six, to achieve the maximum of effectiveness – and also of precision.

But Lenin was not just a volcano: his brain worked like a laboratory of revolution, an exact, scientific machine which refused to take account of expectations or hopes. Sometimes, in situations of extreme tension, he was reluctant to acknowledge the unfavourable results of a first test; he would cursorily reject the evidence, would identify himself with the situation still more completely than before, refuse to regard its possibilities as exhausted, try to persuade himself and others that, given sufficient will-power, the desired aim could still be achieved despite the discouraging evidence. At such moments Lenin dismissed every objection, waged polemics of the utmost vehemence against anyone who held views or advocated tactics different from his own, and abused his opponents with astonishing rudeness (his epigones, so unlike him in every other respect, have eagerly appropriated this method of argument). Yet Lenin the 'voluntarist', while trying to extract the impossible from a given situation, had his ear finely attuned to reality at the same time; he would observe the attitude of the mass of workers and peasants, register every change in their reaction to events, every modification in the relationship of social forces, and then, suddenly, he would swing the helm right round and decide upon a retreat, a compromise, a strategic withdrawal.

Lenin never considered himself infallible; he was not interested in what other politicians call 'prestige' – the loss of which they dread far more than the consequences of clinging to a false decision. He was able to combine impetuous boldness with cautious circumspection, radicalism with realism. He did not shrink from harsh words, yet he abhorred revolutionary phrase-mongering. Obsessed by his cause, yet never divorced from reality (reality seen not as a momentary set of circumstances such as can be expressed in statistical terms, but as a complex dynamic process made up of many different factors and carrying within itself the seeds of an as yet uncreated future), he often overrode the majority at moments of decision – for example, on 16 April 1917, directly after his arrival in St Petersburg, when he proclaimed the change-over from a bourgeois to a proletarian revolution, or directly before the armed insurrection in October 1917, or during the peace negotiations of Brest-Litovsk in February 1918. In such situations he was harshly impatient of old companions-in-arms if they opposed him; yet, having overridden them, he was able to draw them back into the struggle. He collaborated with revolutionaries of many persuasions, and could weld them into a strong fighting community while respecting their individual outlooks. Even after the fateful decision of the Tenth Bolshevik Party Congress (8–12 March 1921) proclaiming the 'mono-lithic' nature of the Party and prohibiting factions within it, Lenin did not put a stop to open discussion within the Party: he demanded discipline, not regimentation.

Although he saw the contradiction between word and deed as one of the worst vices of bourgeois society and proclaimed the unity of theory and practice as the essential feature of scientific revolutionary socialism, Lenin not infrequently found himself in situations where the balance of theory and practice was extremely precarious. Like every great revolu-tionary, he tended to overestimate the rate of revolutionary development and expected results in a matter of days or weeks when in fact they could hardly be achieved within a decade. In his impatience to speed up practice, he sometimes adapted his theories to the impetus of his own personality and the demands of his immediate aims. 'At the beginning was the Deed.' These words of Goethe's Faust apply to no other man so much as they do to Lenin.

Marx was concerned above all with revolutionary cognition, Lenin with revolutionary action.

In the 1920s El Lissitsky, the Russian 'formalist' artist, designed a monument which was genuinely expressive of Lenin's genius. It was a steel construction rather like a wireless transmitter projecting diagonally into space, a symbol of the century of scientific and technical achievement. Unlike the leaning tower of Pisa, this slender metal tower is not at rest; it has the dynamism of a piece of work in progress, a catapult about to hurl a projectile into the world. This projectile, on a platform jutting forward as though about to take off, is Lenin;

he appears to be repeating the vehement motion of the catapult, perhaps even to be causing it. One feels that at any
moment this projectile will fly off into the unknown, into a
near or distant future, into days and years that will shake the
world.

ON S'ENGAGE

Marx and Engels adopted Hegel's view that history is not just a random series of conceited actions by conceited men, an accumulation of mere facts, a meaningless sequence of unrelated events. But they went further than Hegel, who was content to see through the multicoloured crust of appearances in order to comprehend and render conscious the nature of historical development. Proceeding from discovered laws of history, Marx and Engels saw that it was necessary to create change, to shake all petrified social relations by exposing the untenable contradictions and the potentialities within them. They were convinced that the conditions in which men live and earn their living are largely determined by who owns the principal means of production, and that production relations must, in the last analysis, correspond to the development of the productive forces, the tools and instruments men make in their effort to dominate nature, the methods, experiences and forms of labour, the knowledge and the insights of man.

It is true that sometimes, in order to accentuate the meaning of their new theory, Marx and Engels compared the working of this law of historical motion with a process in natural history; yet they pointed out often enough that the greatest caution is needed in drawing comparisons between historical tendencies and natural laws. Men are the vectors of a changing society; they are both the instigators and the agents of social change, both the authors and the actors of the drama of history. Having once come upon the traces of certain laws of motion, they can consciously and scientifically take account of these laws, can work in the same direction as these laws and thus make the birth-pangs of the new society less prolonged and painful.

Marx's and Engels's complex theory of history became the creed of millions of workers who combined their faith in these scientific discoveries with a belief in the inevitability of the Socialist Revolution by means of which capitalist ownership and production would be replaced by a society based upon the socialization of the means of production. Just as capitalism had succeeded feudalism, they believed, so socialism must inevitably follow capitalism. Their teachers' warnings that trends of historical development are not an insurance policy against the forces of barbarism were forgotten, drowned by the battle-cry: 'The world shall be ours despite everything!' In the forward march of the socialist mass movement, Marxism was mechanically simplified and the philosophy of practice was reduced to a soulless fatalism which paralysed free will and responsibility with 'the iron Must of history'. The laws of nature provided the model for the succession of social systems in history. The development towards socialism was considered to be as inevitable, Antonio Gramsci remarked sarcastically at a later time, as the growth of an avalanche; one could sit back and wait for it to happen, secure in the certainty of victory; history was seen as an automatic slot-machine – you put in five liras' worth of industrial capitalism, and five liras' worth of socialism would drop out at the other end.

Thus an institutional ideology came into being which invoked scientific principles but put forward the mystifications of vulgar materialism.

Lenin's significance in the history of theoretical Marxism lies in the fact that, although he was not completely free from the contradictions and errors of his time, he nevertheless successfully revived the notion of Marxism as the *philosophy of practice*. Cognition, decision by free will and the appeal to morality were for him essential elements of a historical necessity which does not operate independently from men but embraces the experiences and decisions of men. Social development, he argued, would proceed victoriously only on the assumption that a constantly increasing number of men would struggle for it. The reproach of voluntarism which was levelled at Lenin even in his lifetime is rooted in a lack of knowledge, or, more often, a lack of comprehension of the nature of the Marxist philosophy of history. But it is an understandable reproach nevertheless. In arguing against the mechanistic and fatalistic views which reduced Marxism to soullessness, Lenin the man of action, the agitator and propagandist, the leader of an active political party, emphasized the will as an important factor more explicitly, more strongly, than did Marx and Engels themselves.

This attitude first found expression when Lenin, then only twenty-four years old, conducted a debate with the so-called 'Narodniks' or 'Populists', who maintained that Russia could by-pass the phase of industrial capitalism and develop socialism out of the remnants of the traditional village commune. In his long pamphlet *What the 'Friends of the People' Are and How They Fight the Social-Democrats* he demonstrated that the phase of industrial capitalism in Russia was already far advanced and could no longer be halted; political slogans, he argued, must be based on scientifically demonstrable facts. Lenin's point of view was not, however – as a Narodnik author wrote – the result of a mechanistic conception of history according to which men are mere puppets mysteriously aroused to life by the immanent laws of historical necessity. The Marxist view of history in no way destroyed

man's reason or conscience, or appraisal of his actions. Quite the contrary, only the determinist view makes a strict and correct appraisal possible instead of attributing everything you please to free will. Similarly, the idea of historical necessity does not in the least undermine the role of the individual in history: all history is made up of the actions of individuals, who are undoubtedly active figures. The real question that arises in appraising the social activity of an individual is: what conditions ensure the success of his actions, what guarantee is there that these actions will not remain an isolated act lost in a welter of contrary acts? This also is a question answered differently by Social-Democrats and by the other Russian socialists: how must actions aimed at bringing about the socialist system attract the masses in order to yield serious fruits? Obviously, the answer to this question depends directly and immediately on the way in which the grouping of social forces in Russia and the class struggle which forms the substance of Russian reality are understood.[2]

Lenin denied the notion that Marxists try to force reality into the Procrustean bed of the theories of Hegel and Marx. Growing industrialization, concentration of capital, socialization of the production process, etc., were objectively and scientifically demonstrable facts and expressed a historical tendency towards a new life order.

... the Marxists unreservedly borrow from Marx's theory only its invaluable methods, without which an elucidation of social relations is impossible, and, consequently, they see the criterion of their judgement of these relations not in abstract schemes and suchlike nonsense at all, but in its fidelity and conformity to reality.[3]

Industrial-capitalist development was progressive compared with barbarian semi-feudal relations, not least because

... it AWAKENS THE MIND OF THE WORKER, converts dumb and incoherent discontent into conscious protest . . .[4]

The theoretical work of socialists had to be directed towards concrete study, their practical work towards helping the workers to assimilate the theory and to find the organization suited to the existing conditions. 'Under these circumstances, theoretical and economic development merge into one,'[5] and 'the direct task of science, according to Marx, is to provide a true slogan of struggle.'[6]

This unity of theory and practice, of slogan and reality, of law and will, formed the basis for the creative interpretation of Marxism which Lenin summed up in an extremely pointed and elliptical formula in his article *Our Programme*, written in exile in 1898, the year of the foundation of the Russian Social-Democratic Labour Party. The real task was not to draw up plans for refashioning society, he wrote, not to preach moral sermons to the capitalists, but

to organize the class struggle of the proletariat and to lead this struggle, the ultimate aim of which is the conquest of political power by the proletariat and the organization of a socialist society.[7]

We do not regard Marx's theory as something completed and inviolable; on the contrary, we are convinced that it has only laid the foundation stone of the science which socialists *must* develop in all directions if they wish to keep pace with life. We think that an *independent* elaboration of Marx's theory is especially essential for Russian socialists; for this theory provides only general *guiding* principles, which, in *particular*, are applied in England differently than in France, in France differently than in Germany, and in Germany differently than in Russia.[8]

Later, when the practice of quoting from Lenin was carried to excess, these sentences were seldom recalled.

It was in the specific context of Russian politics, and more especially in his famous work *What Is To Be Done?*, that Lenin emphasized the factor of the will. This epoch-making book was written at the beginning of 1902 in the debate with the so-called 'Economists', a Russian variety of the revisionism

represented by the German Social-Democrat Eduard Bernstein, whose basic idea was summed up in the dictum: 'The
aim is nothing, the movement is all.' The 'Economists' in
Russia recommended that the workers should confine themselves to the economic and trade union aspect of the struggle,
which would sooner or later yield political results satisfactory
to both the Marxist intellectuals and the liberal bourgeoisie.
This doctrine, which relied entirely upon the spontaneous
movement of the masses, was based on a belief in automatic
laws of social development.

Lenin argued, on the contrary, that the significance of
Marxist theory consisted precisely in looking ahead and
developing the right strategy of struggle. Hence there could
not be a revolutionary movement without revolutionary theory,
and only a party guided by a revolutionary theory could play
the part of a vanguard in the struggle, the more so as history
had confronted the Russian working class with an immediate
task 'which is the *most revolutionary* of all the *immediate* tasks
confronting the proletariat of any country'.[9] To train the
working class in conscious struggle, to develop its revolutionary consciousness, was the most important task for a
Marxist. The spontaneous element of the mass struggles of the
1890s had been 'consciousness in embryonic form'. Later there
had been 'far greater flashes of consciousness ... the systematic strikes represented the class struggle in embryo ... but
the workers were not, and could not be, conscious of the
irreconcilable antagonism of their interest to the whole
modern political and social system.' The spontaneous element
was still predominant because the struggle was still primarily a
trade union one, not a socialist one. A socialist consciousness
could be introduced into the working class only from the outside – to be precise, only by Marxist intellectuals.

The history of all countries shows that the working class,

exclusively by its own effort, is able to develop only trade-union consciousness, i.e., the conviction that it is necessary to combine in unions, fight the employers, and strive to compel the government to pass necessary labour legislation, etc. The theory of socialism, however, grew out of the philosophic, historical, and economic theories elaborated by educated representatives of the propertied classes, by intellectuals. By their social status, the founders of modern scientific socialism, Marx and Engels, themselves belonged to the bourgeois intelligentsia.[10]

Political consciousness was not an automatic product of economic struggle. The workers were dominated by bourgeois ideology, which was far older than socialist ideology and had immeasurably greater means of dissemination at its disposal. The working class gravitated spontaneously towards socialism, but Marxist intellectuals could not rely on this spontaneity and trot at the heels of events as 'simple servants of the working-class movement'. That would be a negation of all strategy and all tactics.

It means belittling the initiative and energy of class-conscious fighters, whereas Marxism, on the contrary, gives a gigantic impetus to the initiative and energy of the Social-Democrat, opens up for him the widest perspectives, and (if one may so express it) places at his disposal the mighty force of many millions of workers 'spontaneously' rising for the struggle.[11]

The role of revolutionaries did not, therefore, consist in relying upon spontaneous movement; by analysing not only the economic aspect but all aspects of social life, they must develop the social consciousness of the masses; they must convince the masses of the necessity for revolutionary activity, not only in relation to immediate economic questions but by exposing also the brutal methods of the police, the persecution of religious sects, the flogging of peasants, the ill-treatment of soldiers, the repression of the most innocent cultural activities.

29

The task of the Social-Democrats, however, is not exhausted by political agitation on an economic basis; their task is *to convert* trade-unionist politics into Social-Democratic political struggle, *to utilize* the sparks of political consciousness which the economic struggle generates among the workers, for the political purpose of *raising* the workers to the level of *Social-Democratic* political consciousness.[12]

Thus it was the duty of Marxist intellectuals to pass on political knowledge to the workers and to refuse to regard politics as the domain of an intellectual elite. The ideal leader was not a trade-union secretary content with assisting the workers in the economic struggle.

It cannot be too strongly maintained that *this is still not* Social-Democracy, that the Social-Democrat's ideal should not be the trade-union secretary, but the *tribune of the people*, who is able to react to every manifestation of tyranny and oppression, no matter where it appears, no matter what stratum or class of the people it affects; who is able to generalize all these manifestations and produce a single picture of police violence and capitalist exploitation; who is able to take advantage of every event, however small, in order to set forth *before all* his socialist convictions and his democratic demands, in order to clarify for *all* and everyone the world-historic significance of the struggle for the emancipation of the proletariat.[13]

Marxist intellectuals had failed to cope with that task because they lacked adequately trained organizers and leaders who might have enabled them to become the spearhead of the movement. Inept amateurishness in organizational matters was merely encouraged by the worship of spontaneity which led to 'gazing with awe upon the posterior of the Russian proletariat'. Organizing was an art like any other. If the intention was to raise the workers to the level of revolutionaries, then it was essential that revolutionaries should not be reduced to the status of mere amateurs.

The entire range of ideas of *What Is To Be Done?*, the most important work in the history of Marxism opposing the fatalist interpretation of scientific socialism, is summed up in the celebrated sentence: 'Give us an organization of revolutionaries and we will overturn Russia.'[14] Revolutionaries should dream of such an organization. 'I wrote these words and became alarmed,' Lenin confesses, and then goes on to formulate a possible objection:

'I ask, has a Marxist any right at all to dream, knowing that according to Marx mankind always sets itself the tasks it can solve?' and replies: 'I shall try to hide behind the back of Pisarev . . . The rift between dreams and reality causes no harm if only the person dreaming believes seriously in his dream, if he attentively observes life, compares his observations with his castles in the air, and if, generally speaking, he works conscientiously for the achievement of his fantasies.'

And Lenin adds: 'Of this kind of dreaming there is unfortunately too little in our movement. And the people most responsible for this are those who boast of their sober views, their "closeness" to the "concrete".'[15]

Twenty years later H. G. Wells was to call Lenin 'the dreamer in the Kremlin'.

Thus it was completely in tune with his philosophical interpretation of Marxism, his refusal to let the power of free decision, the possibility of an alternative, the force of the human conscience, be crushed by the iron laws of history, when, in the first Russian revolution of 1905, after the suppression of the Moscow rising, Lenin concentrated his autocriticism upon the inadequate organizational preparedness of the Party – upon the missed opportunities, the failure to find the right solution and the right organizational form in the right situation.

Thus, nothing could be more short-sighted than Plekhanov's

view, seized upon by all the opportunists, that the strike was untimely and should not have been started, and that 'they should not have taken to arms'. On the contrary, we should have taken to arms more resolutely, energetically and aggressively; we should have explained to the masses that it was impossible to confine things to a peaceful strike and that a fearless and relentless armed fight was necessary.[16]

'Let us remember that a great mass struggle is approaching. It will be an armed rising.'[17]

A decade later, after the victory of the armed insurrection, when, in the backward, semi-barbarian country that was Russia, a country devastated by war and civil strife, the difficulties confronting the victorious revolution had grown to gigantic proportions, when, in face of these difficulties, the mechanistic interpreters of Marxism argued that revolution in a backward country contradicted all Marx's ideas and that the stage of semi-feudal tsarism should have been followed by a prolonged phase of industrial capitalism, Lenin – by that time fatally ill – once more, only a year before his death, summed up the different interpretations and applications of Marxism in the following terms:

They all call themselves Marxists, but their conception of Marxism is impossibly pedantic. They have completely failed to understand what is decisive in Marxism, namely, its revolutionary dialectics. . . .
. . . they are complete strangers to the idea that while the development of world history as a whole follows general laws it is by no means precluded, but, on the contrary, presumed, that certain periods of development may display peculiarities in either the form or the sequence of this development . . .
Infinitely stereotyped, for instance, is the argument they learned by rote during the development of West-European Social-Democracy, namely, that we are not yet ripe for socialism, that, as certain 'learned' gentlemen among them put it, the

objective economic premises for socialism do not exist in our country. It does not occur to any of them to ask: but what about a people that found itself in a revolutionary situation such as that created during the first imperialist war? Might it not, influenced by the hopelessness of its situation, fling itself into a struggle that would offer it at least some chance of securing conditions for the further development of civilization that were somewhat unusual? . . .

What if the complete hopelessness of the situation, by stimulating the efforts of the workers and peasants tenfold, offered us the opportunity to create the fundamental requisites of civilization in a different way from that of the West-European countries? . . .

If a definite level of culture is required for the building of socialism (although nobody can say just what that definite 'level of culture' is, for it differs in every West-European country), why cannot we begin by first achieving the prerequisites for that definite level of culture in a revolutionary way, and *then*, with the aid of the workers' and peasants' government and the Soviet system, proceed to overtake the other nations? . . .

Napoleon, I think, wrote: *'On s'engage et puis . . . on voit.'* Rendered freely this means: 'First engage in a serious battle and then see what happens.' Well, we did first engage in a serious battle in October 1917 . . .

Our European philistines never even dream that the subsequent revolutions in Oriental countries, which possess much vaster populations and a much vaster diversity of social conditions, will undoubtedly display even greater distinctions than the Russian revolution.[18]

2

THE PARTY

We have shown that when Lenin emphasized the importance of the revolutionary organization, the revolutionary party, this was in line with the logic of his historico-philosophical interpretation of Marxism and his concept of the role of the subjective factor in social development. 'Before us,' he wrote, in all its strength, towers the enemy fortress which is raining shot and shell upon us, mowing down our best fighters. We must capture this fortress, and we will capture it, if we unite all the forces of the Russian revolutionaries into one party which will attract all that is vital and honest in Russia.

We find these words in the first issue of the paper *Iskra* – 'The Spark' – which first appeared in December 1900 and whose motto was taken from the Decembrists' reply to a greeting sent them by Pushkin: 'From this spark will come a blaze.' With his characteristic skill – to use his own metaphor – of finding the essential link which, in every situation, holds together the whole chain, Lenin had recognized that the creation of a central all-Russian revolutionary newspaper was a decisive step towards overcoming the fragmentation and diffuseness of the Russian labour movement, as well as its tendency towards individual acts of terrorism. The paper would not only act as collective propagandist and agitator, but also as collective organizer, since a whole network of reliable men, a 'regular army of tried fighters', would be needed to produce and distribute it.

This newspaper would become part of an enormous pair of smith's bellows that would fan every spark of the class struggle and of popular indignation into a general conflagration.[19]

It is true that the accentuation of the subjective factor was here combined with the conclusions which Lenin drew from the specifically Russian conditions of political struggle – the illegal status of the labour movement and its persecution by the tsarist police.

We are marching in a compact group along a precipitous and difficult path, firmly holding each other by the hand. We are surrounded on all sides by enemies, and we have to advance almost constantly under their fire. We have combined, by a freely adopted decision, for the purpose of fighting the enemy, and not of retreating into the neighbouring marsh, the inhabitants of which, from the very outset, have reproached us with having separated ourselves into an exclusive group and with having chosen the path of struggle instead of the path of conciliation.[20]

The 'compact group' had to acquire revolutionary experience and organizing skill; it had to be filled with the will to develop these necessary qualities and to recognize the mistakes which had previously put them out of its reach. These demands could be satisfied only by professional revolutionaries, since the illegal struggle against the political police had to be organized 'according to all the rules of the art' by men for whom revolutionary work had become a profession. Within the organization of professional revolutionaries all distinctions between workers and intellectuals must be effaced. The illegal group, which had to be as well trained as the police, would centralize all conspiratorial activities; in face of the difficult conditions of clandestinity, group democracy (or 'democratism') was nothing more than a useless or harmful toy, and the invocation of 'democratism' was a specifically foreign (i.e., non-Russian) argument. A revolutionary organization could not, with the best will in the world, afford the luxury of broad democracy. This would only aid the police in carrying out mass arrests and would perpetuate the amateurishness so characteristic of the Russian labour movement which had prevented the training of professional revolutionaries.

The only serious organizational principle for the active workers of our movement should be the strictest secrecy, the strictest selection of members, and the training of professional revolutionaries. Given these qualities, something even more than 'democratism' would be guaranteed to us, namely, complete, comradely, mutual confidence among revolutionaries.[21]

The quarrel which broke out a year later, at the Second Party Congress of the League of Russian Social-Democrats Abroad, over paragraph I of the Party rules, could appear as an incomprehensible wrangle only to West Europeans; from the Russian point of view it was a fair reflection of two conflicting interpretations of Marxism. At this congress, where the terms 'Mensheviks' (members of the minority) and Bolsheviks (members of the majority) were coined, Lenin proposed that a Party member should be defined as one who accepted the Party programme, supported the Party financially, and belonged to one of its organizations. The counter-proposal was to replace the condition of belonging to a Party organization by that of *working under the control* of one of the Party organizations. On this issue, the Bolsheviks (majority group) were defeated. When after the Party congress, *Iskra* was taken over by the Mensheviks, Lenin wrote *One Step Forward, Two Steps Back* (1904). This work, together with *What Is To Be Done?*, is regarded as the fundamental ideological and organizational exposé of Bolshevism – with some justification, since Lenin believed that differences of opinion on organizational matters were a direct expression of ideological differences. What was Lenin's object in introducing his proposal?

I thereby express clearly and precisely my wish, my demand, that the Party, as the vanguard of the class, should be as *organized* as possible, that the Party should admit to its ranks only such elements *as allow of at least a minimum of organization.* My opponent, on the contrary, *lumps together* in the Party organized and unorganized elements, those who lend themselves to direction and those who do not, the advanced and the incorrigibly backward – for the corrigibly backward can join an organization.[22]

The Party was the vanguard of the working class, and therefore a distinction had to be drawn between those who belonged to the Party and those who occasionally supported it; this distinction corresponded to the degree of consciousness and activity of the persons concerned. The following categories then emerged from the conditions of conspiratorial work and revolutionary struggle: the organization of professional revolutionaries and revolutionary workers, who formed the Party; workers' organizations which were supported by the Party; workers' organizations which submitted to the Party's control; unorganized elements which, at times of acute struggle, placed themselves under the Party's leadership. In his polemic against the charge of centralism and anti-democratism, Lenin, who in *What Is To Be Done?* had emphasized the avant-garde role of Marxist intellectuals, now championed proletarian organization and discipline against the individualism of the intellectuals. It was sheer intellectual opportunism, he wrote, to demand autonomy in organizational matters from the central Party authority and thus to weaken the influence of the revolutionary organizations.

Let me tell you gentlemen who are so solicitous about the younger brother that the proletariat is not afraid of organization and discipline! The proletariat will do nothing to have the worthy professors and high-school students who do not want to join an organization recognized as Party members merely because they work under the control of an organization. The proletariat is trained for organization by its whole life, far more radically than many an intellectual prig.[23]

This aristocratic anarchism is particularly characteristic of the Russian nihilist. He thinks of the Party organization as a monstrous 'factory'; he regards the subordination of the part to the whole and of the minority to the majority as 'serfdom' (see Axelrod's articles); division of labour under the direction of a centre evokes from him a tragicomical outcry against transforming people into 'cogs and wheels' . . .[24]

Lenin, the man of extreme situations, was in the habit of making extreme statements and of over-stressing contradictions when engaged in a polemic. Thus, in rebutting the charge of bureaucratism, he wrote:

Bureaucracy versus democracy is in fact centralism versus autonomism; it is the organizational principle of revolutionary Social-Democracy as opposed to the organizational principle of opportunist Social-Democracy. The latter strives to proceed from the bottom upward, and, therefore, wherever possible and as far as possible, upholds autonomism and 'democracy', carried (by the overzealous) to the point of anarchism. The former strives to proceed from the top downward, and upholds an extension of the rights and powers of the centre in relation to the parts.[25]

This statement, which applied to the conditions prevailing in Russia at the time, formed part of a general struggle against anarchistic tendencies and was specifically adapted to the needs of a young, illegal party, was later, under completely different circumstances, misused in a most harmful way, although Lenin, in the same work, made it clear that he was against bureaucratism in the usual sense of the word.

Lenin's aim in 1904 was to translate into practical, organizational action his belief that objective laws of social development have to be realized through free decision and determined struggle. Social development was not automatically assured; a step forward could be followed by two steps back. But:

In its struggle for power the proletariat has no other weapon but organization. Disunited by the rule of anarchic competition in the bourgeois world, ground down by forced labour for capital, constantly thrust back to the 'lower depths' of utter destitution, savagery, and degeneration, the proletariat can, and inevitably will, become an invincible force only through its ideological unification on the principles of Marxism being reinforced by the material unity of organization, which welds millions of toilers into an army of the working class. Neither the senile rule of the Russian autocracy nor the senescent rule of international capital will be able to withstand this army. It will more and more firmly close its ranks, in spite of all zig-zags and backward steps, in spite of the opportunist phrase-mongering of the Girondists of present-day Social-Democracy, in spite of the self-satisfied exaltation of the retrograde circle spirit, and in spite of the tinsel and fuss of *intellectualist* anarchism.[26]

Lenin accepted the charge of Jacobinism as a compliment because he believed in a tightly knit, centrally controlled organization whose aim was to lead large popular masses into the struggle under conditions of illegality. When, in 1905, the first Russian revolution had created the possibilities for a democratic, legal working-class movement, Lenin did not hesitate to announce to the Party organizations that the suffocating period of illegality was now over and the principle of democratic elections had to be applied; however, certain precautionary measures still had to be maintained in case the Party was once more declared illegal. The democratic interlude lasted only for a brief period, the revolution was crushed; when, in 1912, the Bolsheviks formed an independent party of their own, their insistence on the need for a tightly controlled illegal party was a major argument against the 'liquidators'.* The outbreak of war confirmed them in the conviction that conspiratorial, illegal forms of organization were necessary because this organizational principle was now no longer confined to Russia. The Bolsheviks, who, after the victory of the October Revolution, dropped the name of Social-Democrats and re-named themselves Communists, and who, in March 1919, took the initiative of founding a Communist International, recommended to the new Communist Parties the adoption not only of the political and organizational experience of the victorious mother Party, but also of its organizational rules.

The problems which arose from the fact that ideas and practices which had been adopted under specifically Russian conditions now had to be applied in other countries and under different circumstances did not become immediately and powerfully apparent, because the Bolshevik Party in its early days had developed in an atmosphere of inner-party democracy. On a number of occasions Lenin himself had been outvoted, and extremely controversial views had often been expressed in a Party organ specially provided for the purpose of free discussion. Lenin stated explicitly that the opposition within the Party had 'extremely sound aspirations, trend and programme'.[27]

But these problems became clearer when the Tenth Bolshevik Party Congress in March 1921, after a long and vehement discussion on the problem of the trade unions, prohibited the formation of factions and groups with platforms of their own within the Party and when the Communist International, as a 'world Party', made this principle binding upon all member Parties. Lenin believed, however, that this principle

* The group which wanted to replace the illegal party by an 'open workers' party'. – *Trans.*

could be combined with a maximum of information and discussion within the Party.

All members of the Party must make a calm and painstaking *study* of (1) the essence of the disagreements and (2) the development of the Party struggle. A study must be made of both, because the essence of the disagreements is revealed, clarified and specified (and very often transformed as well) in the *course of the struggle*, which, passing through its various stages, always shows, at every stage, a *different* line-up and number of combatants, *different* positions in the struggle, etc. A *study* must be made of both, and a demand made for the most exact, printed documents that can be thoroughly verified. Only a hopeless idiot will believe oral statements.[28]

3

THE THEORY OF REVOLUTION

Convinced as he was that Marxism is not a closed system and that Russian Marxists should develop Marxism in accordance with the special conditions of their country, Lenin expanded, retouched and modified the theories of revolution put forward by the founders of scientific socialism. But we should add that for a long time he believed he was proceeding within the framework of Marx's model of revolution – until the quantity of changes and corrections he introduced was transformed into the quality of a new model.

Marx and Engels had expected the socialist revolution, the seizure of power by the proletariat, to occur as an essentially simultaneous event in the developed capitalist countries of the West, without excluding the possibility that the initial spark might be struck in a backward country where the bourgeois revolution was carried out under more advanced conditions and with a more developed proletariat than had been the case in England in the seventeenth century or in France in the eighteenth century. If this were to occur, the bourgeois revolution in the more backward country would serve as the immediate prelude to a proletarian one, which in turn would occur within the framework of the general socialist revolution of the developed capitalist countries of the West. For this reason, the *Communist Manifesto*, published on the eve of the Revolution of 1848, turned its attention chiefly to Germany;

and, for the same reason, after the defeat of the German working-class movement in the 1848 Revolution, Marx and Engels wanted, in the event of the seizure of power by a petty-bourgeois democracy, to proclaim the revolution in permanence and to drive it forward and onward on the assumption that this revolutionary development would coincide with a direct victory of the working class in France, which was more highly developed. This was the reason, too, why Marx and Engels in the 1880s saw Russia as the vanguard of revolutionary activity in Europe. Russia, on the eve of a bourgeois-democratic revolution, would carry out that revolution under much more advanced conditions and with a far more developed proletariat than had been the case in all previous bourgeois revolutions; hence the bourgeois-democratic revolution in Russia might become the signal for a proletarian revolution in the West, which in turn would influence the development of Russia's socialist revolution.[29]

At first, Lenin completely accepted these ideas. After the Russian Revolution of 1905 had broken out, but before the insurrection of the sailors on the battleship *Potemkin*, he concluded that a real bourgeois revolution in Russia could occur only under the leadership of the proletariat. In face of the already developed proletariat, he argued, the Russian bourgeoisie was not interested in a consistent revolution; the bourgeois-democratic revolution – the overthrow of tsarism and agrarian revolution – had to be carried out by force of arms and in close alliance with the broad masses of the peasantry, and its outcome would be a revolutionary-democratic dictatorship of workers and peasants. On the ground thus won, the working class, allied with the semi-proletarian strata of the rural population, would begin the struggle for a socialist revolution. The bourgeois-democratic revolution in Russia would act as a pilot light for a socialist revolution in the West, which in turn would facilitate the struggle for socialism in Russia. The important text in which Lenin developed these ideas is entitled *Two Tactics of Social Democracy in the Democratic Revolution*. In it he puts forward the Bolshevik point of view, as distinct from the ideas of the Mensheviks, and he goes further than Marx's and Engels's belief that the unused reserve of bourgeois revolutions can become a potential force in a socialist revolution.

The starting-point of Lenin's argument was as follows: the outcome of the revolution then in progress (the manuscript was completed in July 1905) would depend on whether the working class remained a subsidiary of the bourgeoisie or played the part of leader of the people's revolution. The liberal bourgeoisie was seeking a compromise with the Tsar; it feared every revolutionary development. The Social-Democratic party must therefore orient itself towards armed insurrection and the formation of a provisional revolutionary government, and, as the organ of the victorious insurrection, it must guarantee the most far-reaching democracy. The immediate proclamation of a socialist revolution, as proposed, for example, by the anarchists, would be completely at variance with the degree of Russia's economic development and the degree of class-consciousness and organization of the working class. 'Whoever wants to reach socialism by any other path than that of political democracy, will inevitably arrive at conclusions that are absurd and reactionary both in the economic and the political sense.'[30]

The Mensheviks' slogan of a bourgeois revolution under the leadership of the bourgeoisie was seen by Lenin as typical of their fundamentally different interpretation of Marxism.

Good marchers but poor leaders, they disparage the materialist conception of history by ignoring the active, leading, and guiding part which can and must be played in history by parties that have realized the material prerequisites of a revolution and have placed themselves at the head of the progressive classes.[31]

The two different tactics corresponded to two different perspectives: on the one hand, a *bourgeois revolution* strangled by a compromise between the big bourgeoisie and the Tsar, with the fiction of a constitutional parliament; on the other hand, a *people's revolution*, in which the peasant and proletarian element would predominate. In either case the revolution would be a bourgeois one; it was directed against absolutism and the remnants of feudalism. But the workers had an interest in ensuring that the development of capitalism should proceed not in the Asiatic but in the European way, just as they also had a greater interest than big capital or the landowning magnates in the bourgeois revolution achieving the greatest possible degree of democracy.

In countries like Russia the working class suffers not so much from capitalism as from the insufficient development of capitalism. The working class is, therefore, *most certainly interested* in the broadest, freest, and most rapid development of capitalism. The removal of all the remnants of the old order which hamper the broad, free, and rapid development of capitalism is of absolute *advantage* to the working class. The bourgeois revolution is precisely an upheaval that most resolutely sweeps away survivals of the past, survivals of the serf-owning system (which include not only the autocracy but the monarchy as well), and most fully guarantees the broadest, freest, and most rapid development of capitalism.

That is why a *bourgeois* revolution is *in the highest degree advantageous to the proletariat*. A bourgeois revolution is *absolutely* necessary in the interests of the proletariat. The more complete, determined, and consistent the bourgeois revolution, the more assured will the proletariat's struggle be against the bourgeoisie and for socialism. Only those who are ignorant of the ABC of scientific socialism can regard this conclusion as new, strange, or paradoxical. And from this conclusion, among other things, follows the thesis that *in a certain sense* a bourgeois revolution is *more advantageous* to the proletariat than to the bourgeoisie. This thesis is unquestionably correct in the following sense: it is to the advantage of the bourgeoisie to rely on certain remnants of the past, as against the proletariat, for instance, on the monarchy, the standing army, etc. It is to the advantage of the bourgeoisie for the revolution not to sweep away all remnants of the past too resolutely, but keep some of them, i.e., for this revolution not to be fully consistent, not complete, and not to be determined and relentless . . .

It is of greater advantage to the bourgeoisie for the necessary changes in the direction of bourgeois democracy to take place more slowly, more gradually, more cautiously, less resolutely, by means of reforms and not by means of revolution . . . for these changes to develop as little as possible the independent revolutionary activity, initiative, and energy of the common people, i.e., the peasantry and especially the workers . . . On the other hand it is more advantageous to the working class for the necessary changes in the direction of bourgeois democracy to take place by way of revolution and not by way of reform . . . That is why the more consistent the bourgeois revolution is in achieving its democratic transformations, the less will it limit itself to what is of advantage exclusively to the bourgeoisie. The more consistent the bourgeois revolution, the more does it guarantee the proletariat and the peasantry the benefits accruing from the democratic revolution.[32]

A bourgeois revolution, a bourgeois democracy, yes: but a bourgeois democracy was one thing in England and quite another in Germany.

He would be a fine Marxist indeed, who in a period of democratic revolution failed to see this difference between the degrees of democratism and the difference between its forms.[33]

The Bolsheviks oriented themselves towards a revolution in which the proletariat allied with the peasants would overthrow tsarism and establish a revolutionary-democratic dictatorship of the proletariat and the peasantry. This was not going to be a dictatorship in the usual sense of the word, with the abolition of all democratic freedoms and guarantees, abuse of power, arbitrary rule, etc., that this implied. After a successful insurrection the aim was to create a form of state which would be founded on military force and the armed masses and so could repel the inevitable counter-revolutionary attacks. The aim of such a state would not be to undermine the foundations of capitalism but to bring about a radical re-distribution of landed property and to eradicate the oppressive features of Asiatic bondage in rural and factory life.

Such a victory will not yet by any means transform our bourgeois revolution into a socialist revolution; the democratic revolution will not immediately overstep the bounds of bour-geois social and economic relationships; nevertheless, the significance of such a victory for the future development of Russia and of the whole world will be immense. Nothing will raise the revolutionary energy of the world proletariat so much, nothing will shorten the path leading to its complete victory to such an extent, as this decisive victory of the revolution that has now started in Russia.[34]

To quote Marx, the object was to carry out the bourgeois-democratic revolution 'in the plebeian manner'. The Menshe-viks adopted the position that a bourgeois revolution had to take place under the leadership of the bourgeoisie, and the working-class movement therefore had to be satisfied with the role of a party of extreme opposition. Lenin retorted that categories of the parliamentary struggle in Western Europe should not be applied to revolutions. Neither was it possible to divide revolutionary development into separate stages. Ele-ments of the past and of the future, of bourgeois-democratic revolution and of socialist revolution, were interwoven with one another. In terms of logic it was certainly right to distinguish between periods of development, but in reality certain elements of socialist revolution were already contained in bourgeois-democratic revolutions if these were carried out in the plebeian manner, and, conversely, the future socialist revolution would eventually have to complete a great deal left undone so far as democracy was concerned.

While recognizing the incontestably bourgeois nature of a revolution incapable of *directly* overstepping the bounds of a mere democratic revolution, our slogan *advances* this particular revolution and strives to give it forms most advantageous to the proletariat; consequently, it strives to make the utmost of the democratic revolution in order to attain the greatest success in the proletariat's future struggle for socialism.[35]

In reply to the fears expressed in a Menshevik newspaper that the Bolsheviks' tactics might cause the bourgeois classes to recoil from the revolution and thereby diminish its sweep, Lenin emphasized that the important thing was to win over the peasantry as a wholehearted and radical adherent of the democratic revolution; through this, the sweep of the revolution could only increase.

This is how he summarized the prospects of the revolution at this time:

The proletariat must carry the democratic revolution to completion, allying to itself the mass of the peasantry in order to crush the autocracy's resistance by force and paralyse the bourgeoisie's instability. The proletariat must accomplish the socialist revolution, allying to itself the mass of the semi-proletarian elements of the population, so as to crush the bourgeoisie's resistance by force and paralyse the instability of the peasantry and the petty bourgeoisie.[36]

At the head of the whole people, and particularly of the peasantry – for complete freedom, for a consistent democratic revolution, for a republic! At the head of all the toilers and the exploited – for socialism![37]

The complete victory of the present revolution will mark the end of the democratic revolution and the beginning of a determined struggle for a socialist revolution. Satisfaction of the present-day demands of the peasantry, the utter rout of reaction and the achievement of a democratic republic will mark the utter limit of the revolutionism of the bourgeoisie, and even that of the petty bourgeoisie, and the beginning of the proletariat's real struggle for socialism. The more complete the democratic revolution, the sooner, the more widespread, and the more determined will the development of this new struggle be.[38]

But even such a revolution could serve as a pilot light for the proletarian revolution in the West. Lenin was to remain faithful to this idea of Marx's and Engels's throughout all the modifications of his revolutionary model. When, on 17 October 1905, the Tsar promised a democratic constitution, Lenin commented upon this 'first victory of the revolution' in the following words:

You are not alone, workers and peasants of all Russia! If you succeed in overthrowing, crushing and destroying the tyrants of feudal, police-ridden, landlord and tsarist Russia, your victory will serve as a signal for a world struggle against the tyranny of capital, a struggle for the complete, economic as well as political emancipation of the toilers, a struggle for the deliverance of humanity from destitution, and for the realization of socialism.[39]

This was and remained Lenin's vision when he created a new model of revolution on the basis of successive retouchings, adjustments and corrections of Marx's model.

WAR, IMPERIALISM AND REVOLUTION

The outbreak of the First World War did not immediately cause Lenin to modify his theory. In a declaration on *The War and Russia's Social-Democracy*, written on behalf of the Central Committee in October 1914, he considered that, in view of Russia's extreme backwardness, the principal purpose of a democratic revolution in Russia was to carry the bourgeois revolution through to the end. 'But in all the advanced countries the war has placed on the order of the day the slogan of socialist revolution.'[40] Likewise, the objective defined in the Basle Manifesto of the Socialist International and later abandoned by the Social-Democratic parties – that of making use of the war to overthrow capitalism by revolutionary means – seems to have been restricted in Lenin's mind to the highly developed bourgeois countries. Yet in his polemic against the Social-Democratic party leaderships, which now clamoured in favour of the defence of their respective countries, Lenin came more and more to interpret the Basle Manifesto as binding upon the workers' parties of all countries. In his article *On the Slogan for a United States of Europe*, to which we shall return later, he advanced the following thesis:

Political changes of a truly democratic nature, and especially political revolutions, can under no circumstances whatsoever either obscure or weaken the slogan of a socialist revolution. On the contrary, they always bring it closer, extend its basis, and draw new sections of the petty bourgeoisie and the semi-proletarian masses into the socialist struggle. On the other hand, political revolutions are inevitable in the course of the socialist revolution, which should not be regarded as a single act, but as a period of turbulent political and economic upheavals, the most intense class struggle, civil war, revolutions, and counter-revolutions.[41]

And in an appeal written in the same month (August 1915) he reiterated his conviction that the role of the Russian working-class movement was to serve as 'an example of revolutionary activities' oriented towards an international revolution. The appeal closes with the words: 'Long live the world brotherhood of the workers, and the international revolution of the proletariat!'[42]

A few weeks later he put it still more explicitly: 'Life is *advancing*, through the defeat of Russia, towards a revolution in Russia and, through that revolution and in connection with it, towards a civil war in Europe.'[43]

And in a polemic with Trotsky, whom he accused of denying the possibility of winning over the broad masses of the peasantry, Lenin showed even more clearly how he envisaged the rhythm of development in Russia within the context of the general socialist revolution:

> The proletariat are fighting, and will fight valiantly, to win power, for a republic, for the confiscation of the land, i.e., to win over the peasantry, make *full* use of their revolutionary powers, and get the '*non*-proletarian masses of the people' to take part in liberating *bourgeois* Russia from *military-feudal* 'imperialism' (tsarism). The proletariat will at once utilize this ridding of bourgeois Russia of tsarism and the rule of the landowners, not to aid the rich peasants in their struggle against the rural workers, but to bring about the socialist revolution in alliance with the proletarians of Europe.[44]

Lenin the tactician found his views confirmed by the change in the situation due to the outbreak of war; Lenin the theoretician justified his tactics by the studies on imperialism which he wrote in 1915 and 1916. In Zurich in the spring of 1916 he completed his book *Imperialism, the Highest Stage of Capitalism*, in which he made extensive use of the works of the English economist Hobson (*Imperialism*, 1902) and the Austro-Marxist Hilferding (*Finance Capital*, 1910), but the strategic and tactical conclusions of which were entirely his own and placed his theory of revolution on a new level.

His starting-point was the process of concentration of production, which Marx and Engels had already analysed, and the transformation of the capitalism of free competition into monopoly capitalism ('one of the most important – if not the most important – phenomena of modern capitalist economy'[45]). The breakthrough occurred round the turn of the century. 'The result is immense progress in the socialization of production. In particular, the process of technical invention and improvement becomes socialized.'[46] Within the framework of this process the big banks change their character; they are transformed from pure credit banks into business banks; as such, they dominate whole sections of industry, and the 'personal link-up' between big industry and the big banks is supplemented by the 'personal link-up' between both of them and the government. This coalescence of bank capital with industrial capital (the subject of a brochure by Bukharin for which Lenin wrote the introduction) leads to the formation of a financial oligarchy which controls large sections of the national economy through the system of controlling large holdings of shares. The amount of available capital is further increased by the 'scattering' of shares. Share issues and state loans increase the power and the amount of surplus capital which flows outside the frontiers and extends the financial oligarchy's control to other countries through investments in other (predominantly backward) countries, through loans, etc. The capital-exporting monopolies have divided the world among themselves; international cartels form the basis for international relations, and the economic division of the world provides the ground for the struggle for colonies, spheres of influence, and world domination. But since the world has already been divided up, the struggle naturally becomes one for the *repartitioning* of the world. Agreements between the monopoly unions and the Great Powers are only transitory stages in the process. The transition of capitalism into the stage of monopoly capitalism is connected with an accentuation of the struggle for the re-partitioning of the world.

But – and here we meet one of Lenin's most celebrated theories – the development of individual branches of industry and individual countries, like that of individual enterprises, is uneven and spasmodic.[47] In the re-partitioning of the world, some countries, whose economic potential actually exceeds that of others which have already snatched a large portion of the spoils, are left at a disadvantage. Economic disputes, political conflicts and wars are therefore inevitable. Colonies, which Disraeli had seen as 'millstones round the neck of England', become indispensable for the gigantic monopolies as suppliers of raw materials, opportunities for investment, and spheres of influence. This process involves a whole range of different forms of dependence; in addition to the colonies, there are countries which are politically, formally independent, but which are in reality caught in the mesh of financial and diplomatic dependence.

The non-economic superstructure which grows up on the basis of finance capital, its politics and its ideology, stimulates the striving for colonial conquest. 'Finance capital does not want liberty, it wants domination,' as Hilferding very truly says.[48]

For all these reasons, imperialism represents a special stage of capitalism – namely, the highest stage. It is monopoly capitalism, the transition to a capitalism of a higher order, which is connected with greater socialization of production but also with an aggravation of contradictions, frictions and conflicts. The monopolists assure their profits by corrupting the upper stratum of the proletariat in the developed capitalist countries; this alliance is the soil upon which grows imperialism in general and wartime 'social-imperialism' in particular. The imperialist ideology permeates the working class. Imperialism means reaction all along the line and the intensification of national oppression. It leads to annexations, not only of newly developed countries, but also of older ones.

Lenin's work on imperialism was of particular importance for the theory of revolution because, unlike Marx and Engels, he did not see revolutionary perspectives as centred uniquely upon the advanced capitalist countries. In his remarks concerning uneven development he implied a number of ideas which were to be blown up into a full-scale 'theory' after his death. Thus we read in the already quoted article *On the Slogan for a United States of Europe* (August 1915):

Uneven economic and political development is an absolute law of capitalism. Hence, the victory of socialism is possible first in several or even in one capitalist country alone.

In September 1916, shortly after *Imperialism*, Lenin wrote even more unequivocally in *The Military Programme of Proletarian Revolution*:

The development of capitalism proceeds extremely unevenly in different countries. It cannot be otherwise under commodity production. From this it follows irrefutably that socialism cannot achieve victory simultaneously *in all* countries. It will achieve victory first in one or several countries, while the others will for some time remain bourgeois or pre-bourgeois.[50]

Both passages have become famous because Stalin used them in his polemic against Trotsky to prove that Lenin, too, had believed in the possibility of socialism in one country. Both passages certainly contradict Marx's and Engels's ideas concerning the simultaneous victory of the socialist revolution in the advanced capitalist countries (for it is this which is the point at issue, not the 'building of socialism in one country'); one could certainly call them significant milestones along the path of development of Lenin's theory of revolution. But they are only ideas thrown out without any argumentation to support them. Lenin does not explain precisely why it follows from the uneven development of capitalist commodity production (which, after all, was a fact not unknown to Marx and Engels) that the thesis of the simultaneous victory of the working class in the capitalist countries is untenable.

Lenin never repeated these thoughts because the February Revolution of 1917 and the overthrow of tsarism put him face to face with a new situation. How did the author of the *Two*

Tactics and of *Imperialism* react to the February events? What slogans did the great tactician put forward? To put it briefly, he reacted by going back to the ideas contained in *Two Tactics* and combining them with *Imperialism* and the conclusions he had drawn from the war.

In a lecture on the revolution of 1905 given in January 1917 he had already described that revolution as being a bourgeois-democratic one in its social content but a proletarian one in the weapons it employed: specifically proletarian means of struggle – for example, the strike – had been the distinguishing feature of the revolutionary situation, and Soviets had been created in the factories. In *Letters from Afar*, written after the February Revolution and the overthrow of tsarism, we read: 'The first revolution engendered by the imperialist world war has broken out.'[51] 'The imperialist war was bound, with objective inevitability ... to turn into a civil war between the hostile classes.'[52]

The revolution had been encouraged by a conspiracy between the big industrialists and the capitalist landowners with the allied imperialists who wanted to ensure Russia's continuing participation in the war. The dual nature of the revolution found expression in the dual power established in Russia as its consequence: that of the 'really important' government of the landowners and the bourgeoisie and that of the Soviets, particularly the Petrograd Soviet. What mattered now, said Lenin, was to ensure the complete victory of the republic and to march forward towards socialism in alliance with the proletariats of all the belligerent countries. This was the great task of the Soviets as organs of the insurrection and of revolutionary state power, the Soviets whose victory alone could bring peace to the masses: this was 'our most urgent task'.[53]

In this somewhat modified form of his revolutionary model, the Russian proletariat retained the pioneering role.

To the Russian workers has fallen the honour and the good fortune of being the first to start the revolution – the great and only legitimate and just war, the war of the oppressed against the oppressors.[54]

'Long live the Russian Revolution! Long live the world workers' revolution, which has already begun!' wrote Lenin at the end of a report written at this time: these words show that he considered the Russian Revolution to be part of the international socialism revolution. And in his farewell letter to the Swiss workers, written before his return to Russia, we read once again a summing-up of his view of the international significance of the Russian Revolution:

To the Russian proletariat has fallen the great honour of *beginning* the series of revolutions which the imperialist war has made an objective inevitability. . . . It is not its special qualities, but rather the special conjuncture of historical circumstances that *for a certain, perhaps very short, time* has made the proletariat of Russia the vanguard of the revolutionary proletariat of the whole world.

Russia is a peasant country, one of the most backward of European countries. Socialist *cannot* triumph there *directly* and *immediately*. But the peasant character of the country, the vast reserve of land in the hands of the nobility, *may*, to judge from the experience of 1905, give tremendous sweep to the bourgeois-democratic revolution in Russia and *may* make our revolution the *prologue* to the world socialist revolution, a *step* towards it . . .

Single-handed, the Russian proletariat cannot bring the socialist revolution to a *victorious conclusion*. But it can give the Russian Revolution a mighty sweep that would create the most favourable conditions for a socialist revolution, and would, in a sense, *start* it. It can facilitate the rise of a situation in which its *chief*, its most trustworthy and most reliable collaborator, the *European* and American *socialist* proletariat, could join the decisive battles . . .

The objective circumstances of the imperialist war make it

certain that the revolution will not be limited to the *first* stage of the Russian revolution, that the revolution will *not* be limited to Russia.[55]

The logic of his model of revolution demanded that Lenin should go further than Marx and Engels by speaking of 'world revolution'. He believed that the Russian proletariat, through the first phase of its revolution, had fired the fuse of world revolution.

The notion of a 'fuse', of a 'pilot light', connected Lenin's new model of revolution with Marx's and Engels's model of simultaneous socialist revolution in the advanced capitalist countries. In this notion he concentrated his hope that the international revolutionary movement would help Russia to overcome her difficulties which, because of her initial back-wardness and the devastations of war and civil war, had grown to gigantic proportions. Lenin reckoned on a world revolution occurring within two years of the October Revolution.

'Our struggle is becoming clearer and clearer to the workers of the world, and their mounting indignation is bringing them nearer and nearer to the future revolution,'[56] he said in a speech in January 1918. 'We will fight ... until the international revolutionary proletariat comes to our aid.'[57] 'We are banking on the inevitability of the world revolution, but this does not mean that we are such fools as to bank on the revolution inevitably coming on a *definite* and early date,' he wrote in a letter to American workers in August 1918.

We were only the first country to break the convict chains of the imperialist war.'[58] 'We are now, as it were, in a besieged fortress, waiting for the other detachments of the world socialist revolution to come to our relief. ... Slowly but surely the workers are adopting communist, Bolshevik tactics ... In short, we are invincible, because the world proletarian revolution is invincible.[58]

And in a speech during the same month he said:

Our revolution was begun as a general revolution, and we shall tackle our tasks with the help of the workers and peasants of the world . . . until the world socialist revolution breaks out.[59]

Again in August 1918:

We represent only one detachment, a detachment which has advanced some way ahead of the other workers' detachments – not because it is any better than the others, but because the stupid policy of our bourgeoisie enabled the working class of Russia to throw off its chains sooner . . . But only a fool can ask when revolution will break out in the West.[60]

In November he proposed that stocks of grain should be placed at the disposal of the German workers if, in the course of the coming revolution in their country, they encountered difficulties with food supplies. Revolutionary groups in Western Europe, oriented towards the Bolsheviks, were already being formed. 'World Bolshevism will conquer the world bourgeoisie.'[61]

And when, finally, revolutions broke out in Central Europe in November, he said at a rally in honour of the Austro-Hungarian revolution:

The time is near when the first day of the world revolution will be celebrated everywhere. Our labour and sufferings have not been in vain! The world revolution will triumph! Long live the world proletarian revolution.[62]

The world revolution had begun in a single country, but its triumph was inevitable in the capitalist West as well. In his concluding speech at the closing of the First Congress of the Communist International at the beginning of March 1919 he said: 'The victory of the proletarian revolution on a world scale is assured. The founding of an international Soviet republic is on the way.'[63] The founding of the Communist

International was a significant step towards an international Soviet republic, the victory of the proletariat in the entire world, the World Federative Republic of Soviets.'[64]

The failure of the German revolution was, of course, taken by Lenin as a warning; the German bourgeoisie, he said, showed more intelligence and experience than the stupid Russian bourgeoisie had done. Nevertheless he continued to await the imminent birth of an international Soviet republic. In a draft programme of the Russian Communist Party (Bolsheviks) he wrote that the revolutions in Austria-Hungary and, particularly, in Germany showed vividly that 'the era of the world proletarian, Communist revolution has begun'[65] and that the task of the new Communist parties was to carry out the world revolution. The forming of Béla Kun's government in Hungary seemed to him clear proof of the fact that 'the time is not far distant when Communism will triumph all over the world.'[66] Desperate difficulties – civil war, famine, collapse of the transport system, etc. – had to be surmounted so that 'we shall ... win full victory, so that we shall live to see the day when the world Soviet republic will be added to the Russian and the Hungarian Soviet Republics'.[67] The Third – Communist – International had already begun to develop, to a certain extent, into a union of Soviet Socialist Republics.[68] In a message of greetings to the Hungarian workers on 27 May 1919 he wrote: 'Every month brings the world proletarian revolution nearer'.[69] In July 1919 he concluded his report on the domestic and foreign situation of the Republic to the Moscow Conference of the Party with the confident statement that 'this July will be the last difficult July ... next July we shall welcome the victory of the world Soviet republic, and that victory will be full and complete.'[70]

After the defeat of the Hungarian Soviet Republic Lenin's outlook changed. Occasionally he would still justify the early hope of an imminent world revolution sparked off by the

October Revolution in Russia. The hope had been legitimate, he argued, but it would not be fulfilled as quickly as had been expected. Nevertheless the movement in the West had helped to defeat the intervention of the capitalist countries against the young Soviet state. Russia was only the first contingent of the international proletarian army, and its victory could only be regarded as final when it became part of the victory of the proletariat 'in at least several advanced countries'. It was true, however, that the rate of development was slower than had been hoped.

'We have seen for ourselves that the revolution's development in more advanced countries has proved to be considerably slower, considerably more difficult, considerably more complicated.'[71] Yet, as late as in October 1920, he still considered the British 'Councils of Action' to be the equivalent of Soviets within the framework of a dual power situation.[72]

At this time, Lenin's thoughts on foreign policy and international affairs became dominated to an increasing degree by the problem of peace treaties with the neighbouring states. His ideas on this subject were later reduced, by a process of disingenuous simplification, to suggest that he had believed in a policy of peaceful coexistence. It is true that he was turning increasingly towards a policy of treaties and agreements in the hope of breaking through the international blockade. As well as saluting the solidarity of the international proletariat, he began to pay tribute to the intelligence and realism of the governments of smaller neighbouring countries which established normal relations with the Soviet state. Problems of domestic and economic policy came more and more into the foreground of his thoughts; he insisted that these problems had to be solved to enable the Soviet state to continue in existence while waiting for the world revolution. As far as revolutionary perspectives were concerned, his interest shifted to the national revolutionary movements in the East.

NATION AND REVOLUTION

For a number of years preceding the October Revolution Lenin had recognized that an analysis of the national question in the Russian empire – a close investigation of what was happening to the nations oppressed by the Great-Russians – was urgently needed. The question assumed even greater significance on the eve of the First World War. In his *Critical Remarks on the National Question* (December 1913) Lenin proposed a policy which was by no means automatically shared by all Russian Social-Democrats: no privileges for any one nation or language; complete amalgamation of the workers of all nationalities in all working-class organizations. He rejected the system of 'cultural-national autonomy' advocated by the Austro-Marxists and came out in support of the right of nations to self-determination, including the right of secession. He thought the granting of the franchise to Jews in Russia should head the list of demands contained in a 'bill on the equal rights of nationalities' which the Social-Democrats submitted to the Duma.

A few months later there took place the important debate between Lenin and Rosa Luxemburg, who took the view that in the age of imperialism the slogan of self-determination had lost its meaning because formal political independence could not surmount the economic dependence of small nations on the imperialist Great Powers. In his essay *The Right of Nations to Self-Determination* Lenin conceded that consistent democracy, and therefore also complete national independence, were impossible in the age of imperialism; but that was no reason to abandon the fight for democracy on the widest possible scale, especially as the abandonment of the right of nations to self-determination could only benefit the exploiters of the oppressed peoples of the world. Just as the right to divorce did not signify an obligation to divorce, so the right to self-determination did not imply the obligation to secede. But the socialists of the oppressor nations were precisely the ones who should demand this right if they wished to prevent the working class from being corrupted by nationalism.

In this situation, the proletariat of Russia is faced with a twofold or, rather, a two-sided task: to combat nationalism of every kind, above all, Great-Russian nationalism; to recognize, not only fully equal rights for all nations in general, but also equality of rights as regards polity, i.e., the right of nations to self-determination, to secession. And at the same time, it is their task, in the interests of a successful struggle against all and every kind of nationalism among all nations, to preserve the unity of the proletarian struggle and the proletarian organizations, amalgamating these organizations into a close-knit international association, despite bourgeois strivings for national exclusiveness.[73]

Just because the Great-Russian Social-Democrats loved Russia it was their duty to militate for equal rights of nationalities in order to fight Great-Russian nationalism. In a famous essay entitled *On the National Pride of the Great-Russians*, which Lenin wrote after the outbreak of war in face of the national passions whipped up by demagogues, we read:

Is a sense of national pride alien to us, Great-Russian class-conscious proletarians? Certainly not! We love our language and our country, and we are doing our very utmost to raise *her* toiling masses (i.e., nine-tenths of *her* population) to the level of a democratic and socialist consciousness. To us it is most painful to see and feel the outrages, the oppression and the humiliation our fair country suffers at the hands of the tsar's butchers, the nobles and the capitalists . . .

We are full of a sense of national pride, and for that very

reason we *particularly* hate *our* slavish past (when the landed nobility led the peasants into war to stifle the freedom of Hungary, Poland, Persia and China), and our slavish present, when these selfsame landed proprietors, aided by the capitalists, are leading us into a war in order to throttle Poland and the Ukraine, crush the democratic movement in Persia and China.[74]

His studies on imperialism and his discussions with revolutionary groups at odds with their 'social-patriotic' party leaderships led Lenin to consider the national question directly in a revolutionary perspective. In his theses on *The Socialist Revolution and the Right of Nations to Self-Determination* he defined the slogan of the right of nations to self-determination as one of those democratic demands whose consistent presentation prepared the way for the victory of the proletariat. To abandon this slogan would only help the imperialist oppressors. This was true not only of the colonies, whose insurrections and revolutionary wars had to be supported by all socialists. The condemnation of all annexations made it the duty of socialists to support the right of nations to self-determination.

Lenin rejected the view that national wars could not occur in the age of imperialism and that only civil wars between the proletariat and the capitalist exploiters were possible.

National wars waged by colonies and semi-colonies in the imperialist era are not only probable but *inevitable*. About 1,000 million people, or *over half* of the world's population, live in the colonies and semi-colonies (China, Turkey, Persia). The national liberation movements there are either already very strong, or are growing and maturing. Every war is the continuation of politics by other means. The continuation of national liberation politics in the colonies will *inevitably* take the form of national wars *against* imperialism.[75]

National wars *against* the imperialist powers are not only possible and probable; they are inevitable, progressive and revolutionary.[76]

An important new element was added to Lenin's model of revolution when he wrote, in *The Discussion on Self-Determination Summed Up*:

To imagine that social revolution is *conceivable* without revolts by small nations in the colonies and in Europe, without revolutionary outbursts by a section of the petty bourgeoisie *with all its prejudices*, without a movement of the politically non-conscious proletarian and semi-proletarian masses against oppression by the landowners, the church, and the monarchy, against national oppression, etc. – to imagine all this is to *repudiate social revolution*. So one army lines up in one place and says, 'We are for socialism', and another, somewhere else and says, 'We are for imperialism', and that will be a social revolution! . . . Whoever expects a 'pure' social revolution will *never* live to see it. Such a person pays lip-service to revolution without understanding what revolution is. [77]

After he became the head of the new Soviet state, Lenin did not lose his sympathy for the peoples who had for centuries endured Great-Russian oppression. In 1919 a speech of his on 'Anti-Jewish Pogroms' was recorded on a gramophone record (alas, this record has never been found among the many Lenin recordings made available in later years). In it he said:

Shame on the accursed tsarism which tortured and persecuted the Jews. Shame on those who foment racial hatred towards the Jews, who foment hatred towards other nations. [78]

More poignantly still, we read in some notes which Lenin jotted down during his last illness in December 1922 how he reproached himself with failing to deal quickly and energetically enough with the 'Great-Russian chauvinist' actions of the central Party authorities in Georgia. The following lines are particularly significant:

I suppose I have been very remiss with respect to the workers of Russia for not having intervened energetically and decisively enough in the notorious question of autonomization, which, it appears, is officially called the question of the union of Soviet socialist republics . . .

I have only had time for a talk with Comrade Dzerzhinsky, who came from the Caucasus and told me how this matter stood in Georgia . . .

If matters have come to such a pass that Ordjonikidze could go to the extreme of applying physical violence, as Comrade Dzerzhinsky informed me, we can imagine what a mess we have got ourselves into . . .

It is said that a united apparatus was needed. Where did that assurance come from? Did it not come from that same Russian apparatus which, as I pointed out in one of the preceding sections of my diary, we took over from tsarism and slightly anointed with Soviet oil?

There is no doubt that that measure should have been delayed somewhat until we could say that we vouched for our apparatus as our own. But now we must, in all conscience, admit the contrary: the apparatus we call ours is, in fact, still quite alien to us; it is a bourgeois and tsarist hotch-potch and there has been no possibility of getting rid of it in the course of the past five years without the help of other countries and because we have been 'busy' most of the time with military engagements and the fight against famine.

It is quite natural that in such circumstances the 'freedom to secede from the union' by which we justify ourselves will be a mere scrap of paper, unable to defend the non-Russians from the onslaught of that really Russian man, the Great-Russian chauvinist, in substance a rascal and a tyrant, such as the typical Russian bureaucrat is. There is no doubt that the infinitesimal percentage of Soviet and sovietized workers will drown in that tide of chauvinistic Great-Russian riffraff like a fly in milk . . .[79]

Lenin insisted that practical measures should be taken to protect the Non-Russians within the Soviet Union from the Russian 'Derzhimordas' (bullying officials). In view of the great national-revolutionary movements in the East, the harm that would result from the failure to check such practices would be immense 'not only to us, but to the whole International and to the hundreds of millions of the peoples of Asia, which is destined to follow us on to the stage of history in the near future.'[79]

After the revolutionary tide in Europe had begun to ebb, Lenin came to attach more and more importance to the national revolutionary movements in the colonies and semi-colonies and was more and more preoccupied with the need to speed up revolutionary developments in those countries by modifying the Russian experience – or, as we would put it today, by correcting the Russian model. In an address to the Second All-Russia Congress of Communist Organizations of the Peoples of the East held on 22 November 1919, he said:

The period of the awakening of the East in the contemporary revolution is being succeeded by a period in which all the Eastern peoples will participate in deciding the destiny of the whole world, so as not to be simply objects of the enrichment of others. The peoples of the East are becoming alive to the need for practical action, the need for every nation to take part in shaping the destiny of all mankind . . .

In this respect you are confronted with a task which has not previously confronted the Communists of the world: relying upon the general theory and practice of communism, you must adapt yourselves to specific conditions such as do not exist in the European countries; you must be able to apply that theory and practice to conditions in which the bulk of the population are peasants, and in which the task is to wage a struggle against medieval survivals and not against capitalism.[80]

Lenin now saw the national-revolutionary movements of Asia as a determining part of the world revolution. In a message to an Indian revolutionary association we read:

Only when the Indian, Chinese, Korean, Japanese, Persian

and Turkish workers and peasants join hands and march together in the common cause of liberation – only then will decisive victory over the exploiters be ensured.[81]

At the same time he stressed the fact that these movements were founded on the support of the peasant masses. In the preliminary draft theses on the national and the colonial questions intended for the Second Congress of the Communist International he said that the task was to convince these nations 'that their only salvation lies in the Soviet system's victory over world imperialism'.[82] Almost in the same breath he pointed out that the system of Soviets in these countries would have to be applied to pre-capitalist conditions in which the revolutionary movement was first and foremost a peasant movement, and that the peasants had to be won over to an alliance with the communist proletariat of Western Europe. In a report of the Commission on the National and the Colonial Questions presented to the Second Congress of the Communist International in July 1922 we can already find important elements of the revolutionary model which was later to take shape in the great revolutions of Asia, especially in China and Vietnam. Lenin distinguishes between oppressed and oppressor nations and says that the commission has decided to speak of the national-revolutionary movements in backward countries rather than of a bourgeois-democratic movement. Because the proletariat in these countries was extremely weak, the immediate aim should be the creation of peasants' Soviets.

The national, revolutionary and anti-imperialist movements in Asia increasingly determined the rhythm of world revolutionary development. In an article marking the tenth anniversary of *Pravda*, written at the beginning of May 1922, Lenin wrote:

The basic reason for this tremendous acceleration of world development is that new hundreds of millions of people have been drawn into it. The old bourgeois and imperialist Europe, which was accustomed to look upon itself as the centre of the universe, rotted and burst like a putrid ulcer in the first imperialist holocaust. No matter how the Spenglers and all the enlightened philistines who are capable of admiring (or even studying) Spengler, may lament it, this decline of the old Europe is but an episode in the history of the downfall of the world bourgeoisie, oversatiated by imperialist rapine and the oppression of the majority of the world's population . . .

Meanwhile, India and China are seething. They represent over 700 million people, and together with the neighbouring Asian countries, that are in all ways similar to them, over half of the world's inhabitants. Inexorably and with mounting momentum they are approaching their 1905, with the essential and important difference that in 1905 the revolution in Russia could still proceed (at any rate at the beginning) in isolation, that is, without other countries being immediately drawn in. But the revolutions that are maturing in India and China are being drawn into – have already been drawn into – the revolutionary struggle, the revolutionary movement, the world revolution.[83]

And in the very last article written before his death – *Better Fewer, But Better* – Lenin saw the solution of Russia's difficulties within the context of international revolutionary prospects:

Shall we be able to hold on with our small and very small peasant production, and in our present state of ruin, until the West-European capitalist countries consummate their development towards socialism? But they are consummating it not as we formerly expected . . .

Can we save ourselves from the impending conflict with these imperialist countries? . . . In the last analysis, the outcome of the struggle will be determined by the fact that Russia, China, etc., account for the overwhelming majority of the population of the globe. And during the past few years it is this majority that has been drawn into the struggle for emancipation with extraordinary rapidity, so that in this respect there cannot be the slightest doubt what the final outcome of the world struggle will be. In this sense, the complete victory of socialism is fully and absolutely assured.[84]

Lenin was able to recognize the special importance of the revolutionary potentials of the colonial and semi-colonial countries at least in part because he was profoundly convinced that each nation must move towards socialism 'in its own way', that the increasing multiplicity of the roads to socialism and their 'concrete features' must be respected, that the struggle must inevitably assume special features 'in each country, in conformity with the specific character of its economics, politics, culture, and national composition (Ireland, etc.), its colonies, religious divisions, and so on and so forth.'[85] He rejected all 'stereotyped, mechanically equated, and identical rules of struggle',[86] both in the development towards socialist revolution and after the socialist revolution had taken place.

As long as national and state distinctions exist among peoples and countries – and these will continue to exist for a very long time to come, even after the dictatorship of the proletariat has been established on a world-wide scale – the unity of the international tactics of the communist working-class movement in all countries demands, not the elimination of variety or the suppression of national distinctions (which is a pipe dream at present), but the application of the *fundamental* principles of communism (Soviet power and the dictatorship of the proletariat), which will *correctly modify* these principles in certain *particulars*, correctly adapt and apply them to national and national-state distinctions.[87]

Lenin believed that the Soviets were the universally valid organs of insurrection and power, although the forms in which they appeared would certainly vary from country to country, as he emphasized in a letter of greetings to Hungarian workers.[88] Above all he was entirely convinced that the revolution would assume different forms in different countries. 'The revolution in Italy will run a different course from that in Russia,'[89] he said at the Third Congress of the Communist International. 'It will start in a different way.'[90] The Communist International would never expect Italian workers to 'slavishly copy' the Russian revolution.[91]

4

THE STATE AND REVOLUTION

This was the title Lenin gave to one of his most important books – certainly one of those which had the most far-reaching effects. He wrote it while in hiding, on the eve of the Bolshevik Revolution, during the months of August and September 1917. Its sub-title is: *The Marxist Theory of the State and the Tasks of the Proletariat in the Revolution.* Lenin saw it as his prime task to 're-establish what Marx really taught on the subject of the state'[92] in face of the misrepresentations and distortions practised by the socialist party leaderships. His concern was with the Marxist thesis that the state is an organ of class rule – an instrument for the domination of one class by another; that the liberation of the oppressed class is not possible without the destruction of the state apparatus created by the ruling class; that violent revolution is therefore inevitable and, for that reason, that it is the task of the revolutionary working-class movement to teach the masses to recognize the necessity of violent revolution; that socialist revolution, the smashing of the bourgeois state apparatus, leads to the political rule of the proletariat, which Marx and Engels called the dictatorship of the proletariat. Marx and Engels had thought that violent revolution was inevitable only on the continent of Europe, and that the possibility of a peaceful revolution still existed in England; Lenin argued that, because imperialism had given rise to the creation of a monstrously inflated, repressive state apparatus, England was no longer an exception in that respect.

After the socialist revolution, the bourgeois state would have to be replaced by organizations modelled on the Paris Commune of 1871, 'in which freedom of opinion and discussion does not degenerate into deception, for the parliamentarians themselves have to work, have to execute their own laws, have themselves to test the results achieved in reality, and to account directly to their constituents'.[92]

A community would be created for the first time where the freedom of the oppressors and exploiters would be limited in a number of ways, but where the masses of the poor people would enjoy an expansion of democracy such as had never yet been experienced anywhere; the state would lose its repressive function more and more and would begin to wither away, especially since advanced capitalism would have created the pre-conditions for everyone to be able to take part in the administration of the state. At this point Lenin does more than simply comment on passages from Marx and Engels and draws his own picture of the communist society of the future:

All citizens are transformed into hired employees of the State, which consists of the armed workers. *All* citizens become employees and workers of a *single* country-wide 'syndicate'. All that is required is that they should work equally, do their proper share of work, and get equal pay. The accounting and control necessary for this have been *simplified* by capitalism to the utmost and reduced to the extraordinarily simple operations – which any literate person can perform – of supervising and recording, knowledge of the four rules of arithmetic, and issuing appropriate receipts.

When the *majority* of people begin independently and everywhere to keep such accounts and exercise such control over the capitalists (now converted into employees) and over the intellectual gentry who preserve their capitalist habits, this control will really become universal, general and popular; and there will be no getting away from it, there will be 'nowhere to go'.[93]

Already in his *Letters from Afar*, before his return from Switzerland, Lenin had developed the fundamental notion of people's control over the bureaucracy and the executive, saying that in the future society the poor, exploited sections of the population would actually constitute the organs of state power[94] and the militia of the armed masses would take the place of the executive.[95] Now he describes the transition from the first phase of socialist society, in which to each is given according to his output, to that higher phase of communist society in which the mainsprings of production are already so abundant that to each can be given according to his needs.

From the moment all members of society, or at least the vast majority, have learned to administer the state *themselves*, have taken this work into their own hands, have organized control over the insignificant capitalist minority, over the gentry who wish to preserve their capitalist habits and over the workers who have been thoroughly corrupted by capitalism – from this moment the need for government of any kind begins to disappear altogether. The more complete the democracy, the nearer the moment when it becomes unnecessary. The more democratic the 'state' which consists of the armed workers, and which is 'no longer a state in the proper sense of the word', the more rapidly *every form* of state begins to wither away.

For when *all* have learned to administer and actually do independently administer social production, independently keep accounts and exercise control over the parasites, the sons of the wealthy, the swindlers and other 'guardians of capitalist traditions', the escape from this popular accounting and control will inevitably become so incredibly difficult, such a rare exception, and will probably be accompanied by such swift and severe punishment (for the armed workers are practical men and not sentimental intellectuals, and they will scarcely allow anyone to trifle with them), that the *necessity* of observing the simple, fundamental rules of the community will very soon become a *habit*.[96]

The Paris Commune had shown what steps had to be taken from the start to replace the old bourgeois, repressive state apparatus:

(1) not only election, but also recall at any time; (2) pay not to exceed that of a workman, (3) immediate introduction of control and supervision by *all*, so that *all* may become 'bureaucrats' for a time and that, therefore, *nobody* may be able to become a 'bureaucrat'.[97]

These ideas of Lenin's concerning the withering away of the state confirm that he was proceeding on the assumption that the Russian revolution would be followed quite quickly by more or less simultaneous revolutions in the West.

The State and Revolution is for the most part a concentrated exposé of Marxist doctrine on the state, although Lenin selects only those passages where the Marxist classics speak of the state as a repressive apparatus and where they insist on the necessity for violent revolution. In the extreme situation in which he found himself, Lenin the politician transformed himself into a theoretician, although he was concerned not so much with writing a faultless monograph as with issuing a revolutionary call to action founded solidly upon the ideas of the movement's classics. Marx had allowed for the possibility of a peaceful seizure of power by the proletariat not only in England but also in Holland, and in a number of speeches had referred in general terms to the possibility of socialist revolutions without the use of force; Engels in his criticism of the Erfurt programme of the German Social-Democrats, which Lenin quotes extensively, had even spoken of the possibility of a peaceful revolution in France – the country which, for both Engels and Marx, represented the classic example of that total state machinery which had to be smashed. Lenin dismisses this hypothesis of Engels's by saying that Engels had merely 'conceived' of such a development in France, and puts the word 'conceive' in inverted commas followed by an exclamation mark. Lenin quotes Engels's well-known words to the effect that universal franchise in the state of today could not be anything more than a gauge of the maturity of the working class. Later, however, Engels spoke of universal franchise as a great achievement of the working masses and later still he wrote that universal franchise in the hands of a class-conscious worker was a better weapon than the small-calibre machine-gun in the hands of a trained soldier. And in the last year of his life he described universal franchise as an instrument of liberation of the masses. In another passage, when commenting on Engels's view that the democratic republic is 'the specific form for the dictatorship of the proletariat', Lenin says that what Engels meant by these words was that a democratic republic 'inevitably leads to such an extension, development, unfolding and intensification of the struggle'[98] that it must inevitably lead to the possibility of the dictatorship of the proletariat. Here we cannot help doubting whether this was really the entire meaning of Engels's words. But Lenin was concerned with establishing that in 1917 violent revolution was necessary both in Russia and in the capitalist countries. To establish this, he did not have to revise Marx and Engels – to quote their words was sufficient – but, not being principally a theoretician but a political leader directly engaged in preparing a proletarian revolution, he was somewhat one-sided in his selection of quotations.

In a letter to his friend Inessa Armand, Lenin once wrote: 'Engels was *not* infallible. Marx was *not* infallible.'[99] And so, in his representation of Marx's theory of the state, he went beyond Marx – especially in so far as the development of socialist society after the socialist revolution was concerned. He was not content to base his views on the history of the Paris Commune as commented upon by Marx and Engels, but saw the Soviets of workers', soldiers' and peasants' deputies as the institution which would replace the old machinery of oppression. In his pamphlet *Can the Bolsheviks Maintain State Power?*, written at the end of September 1917, he gives the following reasons for this view:

The Soviets are a new state apparatus which, in the first place provides an armed force of workers and peasants; and this force is not divorced from the people, as was the old standing army, but is very closely bound up with the people. From the military point of view this force is incomparably more powerful than previous forces; from the revolutionary point of view, it cannot be replaced by anything else. Secondly, this apparatus provides a bond with the people, with the majority of the people, so intimate, so indissoluble, so easily verifiable and renewable, that nothing even remotely like it existed in the previous state apparatus. Thirdly, this apparatus, by virtue of the fact that its personnel is elected and subject to recall at the people's will without any bureaucratic formalities, is far more democratic than any previous apparatus. Fourthly, it provides a close contact with the most varied professions, thereby facilitating the adoption of the most varied and most radical reforms without red tape. Fifthly, it provides an organizational form for the vanguard, i.e., for the most class-conscious, most energetic and most progressive section of the *oppressed* classes, the workers and peasants, and so constitutes an apparatus by means of which the vanguard of the oppressed classes can elevate, train, educate and lead *the entire vast mass* of these classes, which has up to now stood completely outside political life and history. Sixthly, it makes it possible to combine the advantages of the parliamentary system with those of immediate and direct democracy, i.e., to vest in the people's elected representatives both legislative *and executive* functions. Compared with the bourgeois parliamentary system, this is an advance in democracy's development which is of world-wide, historic significance.[100]

It must not be overlooked that the Soviets were originally conceived as organs of direct producers' democracy. In the same work Lenin recognized that the state does more than merely exercise repressive functions, and developed certain ideas which we find for the first time in his article *The Impending Catastrophe and How To Combat It*, written a fortnight earlier. In this article n'e had demanded, as the principal immediate measures of control, the amalgamation of all banks into a single nationalized bank, the nationalization of the large industrial trusts, state control over all banking operations and so forth; he had invoked the control measures adopted by states in time of war, and he had envisaged that state monopoly capitalism would offer a material possibility for the transition to socialism. Likewise, we can see by comparing *The State and Revolution* with other works of Lenin's that his views concerning the smashing of the state apparatus were more subtle and more differentiated than is generally thought.

It is true, of course, that Lenin – like Marx and Engels – was convinced that capitalism could not be completely overthrown except by force. He strongly stressed this view in the year 1920 at the Second Congress of the Communist International; yet, in the same year, in a controversy with the Austro-Marxist Otto Bauer, he described the peaceful overthrow of capitalism as 'theoretically possible', if, for example, the workers had already won the battle in nine major capitalist countries and the capitalists in a tenth and smaller country realized the hopelessness of offering further resistance. 'It is quite conceivable that under the circumstances I have mentioned the capitalists in the tenth country, one of the smallest and most "peaceful" countries, might make such a proposal.'[101]

The distinction between Lenin the politician and Lenin the theoretician is demonstrated by the fact that after the February Revolution of 1917 he recommended the peaceful seizure of power by the Soviets as the most painless way, which was worth fighting for with every effort.[102] And when, after August 1917, the left-wing groups within the Petrograd Soviet had joined together to defeat General Kornilov's revolt and certain vacillations among the Mensheviks and the Socialist-Revolutionaries began to be apparent, Lenin once more returned to the possibility of a peaceful revolution. On 27 September (new style) he wrote in *One of the Fundamental Questions of the Revolution*:

> The whole issue at present is whether the petty-bourgeois democrats have learned anything during these great, exceptionally eventful six months. If not, then the revolution is lost, and only a victorious uprising of the proletariat can save it. If they have learned something, the establishment of a stable, unwavering power must be begun immediately.[103]

Agreement between the left parties in the Soviets could ensure a peaceful development of the revolution on the broadest basis and might guarantee a peaceful democratic struggle of parties within the Soviets.

> *Power to the Soviets – this is the only way to make further progress gradual, peaceful and smooth*, keeping perfect pace with the political awareness and resolve of the majority of the people and with their own experience. Power to the Soviets means the complete transfer of the country's administration and economic control into the hands of the workers and peasants, to whom *nobody* would dare offer resistance and who, through practice, through their own experience, *would soon learn* how to distribute the land, products and grain properly.[104]

At the same time, prepared for all eventualities, Lenin wrote from his hiding-place a letter on *Marxism and Insurrection* to the Central Committee of the Party, in which he recalled Marx's dictum that insurrection is an art and that you must win the first success and then proceed from success to success, never interrupting the offensive against the enemy.

> To be successful, insurrection must rely not upon conspiracy and not upon a party, but upon the advanced class. That is the

first point. Insurrection must rely upon a *revolutionary upsurge of the people*. That is the second point. Insurrection must rely upon that *turning-point* in the history of the growing revolution when the activity of the advanced ranks of the people is at its height, and when the *vacillations* in the ranks of the enemy and *in the ranks of the weak half-hearted and irresolute friends of the revolution* are strongest. That is the third point. And these three conditions for raising the question of insurrection distinguish *Marxism from Blanquism*.

Once these conditions exist, however, to refuse to treat insurrection as an *art* is a betrayal of Marxism and a betrayal of the revolution.[105]

All the objective conditions exist for a successful insurrection. We have the exceptional advantage of a situation in which *only* our victory in the insurrection can put an end to that most painful thing on earth, vacillation, which has worn the people out; in which only our victory in the insurrection will give the peasants land immediately; a situation in which *only our* victory in the insurrection can *foil* the game of a separate peace directed against the revolution – foil it by publicly proposing a fuller, juster and earlier peace, a peace that will *benefit* the revolution.[106]

On 9 October Lenin published his article *The Tasks of the Revolution* in which he said once more that the last chance of a peaceful development of the revolution existed if the majority in the Soviets could reach agreement on a concrete programme and if all power were transferred to the Soviets; the Soviets would then immediately propose a general peace to all the belligerent nations, begin the struggle against famine and economic ruin by introducing workers' control over production and distribution, nationalize the banks, the insurance companies and the principal branches of industry and give land to the peasants without requiring compensation.

If the Soviets now take full state power exclusively into their own hands, for the purpose of carrying out the programme set forth above, they will not only obtain the support of nine-tenths of the population of Russia, the working class and an overwhelming majority of the peasantry; they will also be assured of the greatest revolutionary enthusiasm on the part of the army and the majority of the people, an enthusiasm without which victory over famine and war is impossible.

There could be no question of any resistance to the Soviets if the Soviets themselves did not waver. No class will dare start an uprising against the Soviets, and the landowners and capitalists, taught a lesson by the experience of the Kornilov revolt, will give up their power peacefully and yield to the ultimatum of the Soviets. To overcome the capitalists' resistance to the programme of the Soviets, supervision over the exploiters by workers and peasants and such measures of punishing the recalcitrants as confiscation of their entire property coupled with a short term of arrest will be sufficient.

By seizing full power, the Soviets could still today – and this is probably their last chance – ensure the peaceful development of the revolution, peaceful elections of deputies by the people, and a peaceful struggle of parties inside the Soviets; they could test the programmes of the various parties in practice and power could pass peacefully from one party to another.

The entire course of development of the revolution, from the movement of 20 April to the Kornilov revolt, shows that there is bound to be the bitterest civil war between the bourgeoisie and the proletariat if this opportunity is missed. Inevitable catastrophe will bring this war nearer. It must end, as all data and considerations accessible to human reason go to prove, in the full victory of the working class, in that class, supported by the poor peasantry, carrying out the above programme; it may, however, prove very difficult and bloody, and may cost the lives of tens of thousands of landowners, capitalists, and officers who sympathize with them. The proletariat will not hesitate to make every sacrifice to save the revolution, which is possible only by implementing the programme set forth above. On the other hand, the proletariat would support the Soviets in every way if they were to make use of their last chance to secure a peaceful development of the revolution.[107]

Ten days later he called upon the Party leadership to go ahead immediately with organizing the insurrection.

The Bolsheviks are now *guaranteed* the success of the insurrection: (1) we can (if we do not 'wait' for the Soviet Congress) launch a *surprise* attack from three points – from Petrograd, from Moscow and from the Baltic fleet; (2) we have slogans that guarantee us support – down with the government that is suppressing the revolt of the peasants against the landowners! (3) we have a majority *in the country*; (4) the disorganization among the Mensheviks and the Socialist-Revolutionaries is complete; (5) we are technically in a position to take power in Moscow (where the start might even be made, so as to catch the enemy unawares); in Petrograd we could *at once* seize the Winter Palace, the General Staff building, the telephone exchange and the large printing presses. Nothing will be able to drive us out, while agitational work in the *army* will be such as to make it *impossible* to combat this government of peace, of land for the peasants, and so forth.

If we were to attack at once, suddenly, from three points, Petrograd, Moscow and the Baltic fleet, the chances are a hundred to one that we would succeed with smaller sacrifices than on 3–5 July, because *the troops will not advance* against a government of peace.[108]

A week previously, in *Can the Bolsheviks Retain State Power?*, he had ridiculed a 'wealthy engineer' with whom he had had a conversation and who had shied away from the thought of an insurrection as from 'an abyss'. 'He was willing to accept the social revolution if history were to lead to it in the peaceful, calm, smooth and precise manner of a German express train pulling into a station. A sedate conductor would open the carriage door and announce: "Social Revolution Station! *Alles aussteigen!* All change!" '[109] And the pamphlet concludes with the confident assertion that 'no power on earth can prevent the Bolsheviks, *if they do not allow themselves to be scared* and if they succeed in taking power, from retaining it until the triumph of the world socialist revolution.'[110]

On 7 November the Bolsheviks did seize power in an insurrection which claimed only a few victims. The civil war and the Intervention were still to come. But we must not forget that only a few weeks earlier Lenin had not excluded the possibility of a peaceful development.

The state apparatus was by no means completely smashed. What the revolution smashed was, in essence, only the executive – the army and the police apparatus; quite soon Lenin was to complain that tsarist bureaucracy had been driven out of the door but had come back in through the window. The administration was largely formed of the old bureaucracy, thinly disguised beneath a Soviet mask. In his famous letter to the Twelfth Party Congress written in December 1922 – often referred to as Lenin's 'testament' – he said emphatically that 'we took over the old machinery of state from the tsar and the bourgeoisie'.[111] ... 'We inherited it, in effect, from the old regime.'[112]

If the new state power created under Lenin's leadership was unable to throw off the burden of the old bureaucracy, it was the result of Russia's backwardness and terrible devastation.

5

THE DICTATORSHIP OF THE PROLETARIAT

Faithful to the teaching of Marx and Engels, who had anticipated that the socialist revolution would generally occur in the form of a civil war, Lenin defined the state which would come into being after the socialist revolution – ·the state governed by the victorious working class – as a dictatorship of the proletariat, exercising strict control over the defeated exploiting classes and at the same time expanding democracy for the working people to the maximum degree. But he went further than Marx and Engels when he wrote in October 1916:

> . . . Whoever expects that socialism will be achieved *without* a socialist revolution and the dictatorship of the proletariat is not a socialist. Dictatorship is state power based directly on *violence*. And in the twentieth century – as in the age of civilization generally – violence means neither a fist nor a club, but *troops*.[113]

Experience would show the exact nature of this form of government; neither Marx nor the Marxists could foresee every detail, but the direction was clear and so was the role of the separate class forces led by the revolutionary proletariat. The dictatorship of the proletariat would have two aspects – dictatorship *vis-à-vis* the defeated exploiting class and democracy for the working people, this democracy being continuously expanded until the state withered away. Lenin developed the same line of thought, adapting it to the situation immediately preceding the revolution, in *The State and Revolution.*

To confine Marxism to the theory of the class struggle means curtailing Marxism, distorting it, reducing it to something acceptable to the bourgeoisie. A Marxist is solely someone who *extends* the recognition of the class struggle to the recognition of the dictatorship of the proletariat.[114]

Experience of the post-revolutionary period, even in Lenin's lifetime, was to show that these two aspects of the dictatorship of the proletariat were by no means free of contradiction.

In *The Immediate Tasks of the Soviet Government*, written in the spring of 1918, immediately following the revolution, Lenin analysed some of the difficulties facing the young Soviet state. The Bolsheviks' first task had consisted in convincing the majority of the people that the Party's programme and tactics were correct; the next task was to administer the country, backward and devastated as it was, to organize in a new way the economic foundations of the life of scores of millions of people, and, after the relatively easy step of expropriating the bourgeoisie, to assure production and distribution in a new way on the basis of strict accounting and control. Workers' control had to penetrate the consciousness of the people so deeply that discipline and strict accounting would be guaranteed. To assume that such a transition to socialist production could be achieved without dictatorship would be extremely foolish.

On the other hand, it is not difficult to see that during every transition from capitalism to socialism, dictatorship is necessary for two main reasons, or along two main channels. Firstly, capitalism cannot be defeated and eradicated without the ruthless suppression of the resistance of the exploiters, who cannot at once be deprived of their wealth, of their advantages of organization and knowledge, and consequently for a fairly long period will inevitably try to overthrow the hated rule of the poor; secondly, every great revolution, and a socialist revolution in particular, even if there is no external war, is inconceivable without internal war, i.e., civil war, which is even more devastating than external war, and involves thousands and millions of cases of wavering and desertion from one side to another, implies a state of extreme indefiniteness, lack of equilibrium and chaos. And of course, all the elements of disintegration of the old society, which are inevitably very numerous and connected mainly with the petty bourgeoisie (because it is the petty bourgeoisie that every crisis and every war destroys first), are bound to 'reveal themselves' during such a profound revolution. And these elements of disintegration *cannot* 'reveal themselves' otherwise than in increase of crime, hooliganism, corruption, profiteering and outrages of every kind. To put these down *requires time and requires an iron hand.*

There has not been a single great revolution in history in which the people did not instinctively realize this and did not show salutary firmness by shooting thieves on the spot. The misfortune of previous revolutions was that the revolutionary enthusiasm of the people, which sustained them in their state of tension and gave them the strength to suppress ruthlessly the elements of disintegration, did not last long. The social, i.e., the class reason for this instability of the revolutionary enthusiasm of the people was the weakness of the proletariat, which *alone* is able (if it is sufficiently numerous, class-conscious and disciplined) to win over to its side *the majority* of the working and exploited people (the majority of the poor, to speak more simply and popularly) and retain power sufficiently long to suppress completely all the exploiters as well as all the elements of disintegration.

It was this historical experience of all revolutions, it was this world-historic – economic and political – lesson that Marx summed up when he gave his short, sharp, concise and expressive formula: dictatorship of the proletariat. And the fact that the Russian revolution has been correct in its approach to this world-historic task *has been proved* by the victorious progress of the Soviet form of organization among all the peoples and tongues of Russia. For Soviet power is nothing but an organizational form of the dictatorship of the proletariat, the dictatorship of the advanced class, which raises to a new democracy and to independent participation in the administration of the state tens upon tens of millions of working and exploited people, who by their own experience learn to regard the disciplined and class-conscious vanguard of the proletariat as their most reliable leader.[115]

To the extent, however, that the fundamental task of the new state was no longer military suppression but administration, it became more and more important to draw the poor sections of the population into the work of administration – to involve them in the work of the courts, in production control, in ensuring industrial discipline; consequently, the granting of dictatorial powers to individual leaders became necessary. Yet was the appointment of individual dictators with unlimited powers compatible with the fundamental principles of Soviet government? Lenin thought it was. He wrote:

There is, therefore absolutely *no* contradiction in principle between Soviet (that is, socialist) democracy and the exercise of dictatorial powers by individuals. The difference between proletarian dictatorship and bourgeois dictatorship is that the former strikes at the exploiting minority in the interests of the exploited majority, and that it is exercised – *also through individuals* – not only by the working and exploited people, but also by organizations which are built in such a way as to rouse these people to history-making activity. (The Soviet organizations are organizations of this kind.)[116]

All members of the Soviets should be drawn into the practical work of administration. The object was maximum democracy.

Our aim is to draw *the whole of the poor* into the practical work of administration, and all steps that are taken in this direction – the more varied they are, the better – should be carefully recorded, studied, systematized, tested by wider experience and embodied in law. Our aim is to ensure that *every* toiler, having finished his eight hours' 'task' in productive labour, shall perform state duties *without pay*; the transition to this is particularly difficult, but this transition alone can guarantee the final consolidation of socialism.[117]

The contradiction between democracy and dictatorship, workers' control and the dictatorial powers of individuals, remained unsolved and was to play a fateful role in the further development of the Soviet state. The difficulty was increased by the fact that Lenin was forced at an early stage to answer accusations by Social-Democrat politicians and journalists to the effect that the dictatorship of the proletariat in Russia was only a disguise for a rule of terror by a minority. In the *Letter to American Workers*, written on 20 August 1918, he reacts vehemently to this charge:

The British bourgeoisie have forgotten their 1649, the French bourgeoisie have forgotten their 1793. Terror was just and legitimate when the bourgeoisie resorted to it for their own benefit against feudalism. Terror became monstrous and criminal when the workers and poor peasants dared to use it against the bourgeoisie! Terror was just and legitimate when used for the purpose of substituting one exploiting minority for another exploiting minority. Terror became monstrous and criminal when it began to be used for the purpose of overthrowing *every* exploiting minority, to be used in the interests of the vast actual majority, in the interests of the proletariat and semiproletariat, the working class and the poor peasants![118]

The pamphlet *The Proletarian Revolution and the Renegade Kautsky*, written a year after the revolution in reply to Kautsky's brochure *The Dictatorship of the Proletariat*, is devoted in its entirety to refuting this accusation. Lenin refuses to allow the difference between Social-Democrats and Bolsheviks to be presented as the difference between those who believe in democracy and those who believe in dictatorship. The dictatorship of the proletariat is proletarian democracy, bourgeois democracy is the dictatorship of the bourgeoisie. That is the fundamental truth to bear in mind when judging the dictatorship of the proletariat, the key problem of the entire proletarian class struggle. Dictatorship does not necessarily mean the abolition of democracy for the class which exercises dictatorship over other classes; neither does dictatorship in the Marxist sense mean the rule of a single person or group.

Dictatorship is rule based directly upon force and unrestricted by any laws.

The revolutionary dictatorship of the proletariat is rule won and maintained by the use of violence by the proletariat against the bourgeoisie, rule that is unrestricted by any laws.[119]

Bourgeois democracy, although representing a great historical advance over feudalism, is bound to remain restricted, truncated, false and hypocritical under capitalism. All fundamental freedoms are subject to the rule of profit, and whenever a profound political divergence arises, the ruling classes resort to violent action. The so-called equality of bourgeois democracy is subject to a thousand limitations and subterfuges. Parliaments are dominated by banks and stock exchanges. The dictatorship of the proletariat is proletarian democracy; the Soviet Republic, which is just one of its forms, has brought an unprecedented development and expansion of democracy to the exploited working people. It has torn the veil of secrecy from foreign policy, it publishes all secret treaties concerning spheres of influence, and, above all, it enlists the whole people in the work of administration.

The working people are *barred* from participation in bourgeois parliaments (they *never* decide important questions under bourgeois democracy, which are decided by the stock exchange and the banks) by thousands of obstacles, and the workers know and feel, see and realize perfectly well that the bourgeois parliaments are institutions *alien* to them, *instruments for the oppression* of the workers by the bourgeoisie, institutions of a hostile class, of the exploiting minority.

The Soviets are the direct organization of the working and exploited people themselves, which *helps* them to organize and administer their own state in every possible way. And in this it is the vanguard of the working and exploited people, the urban proletariat, that enjoys the advantage of being best united by the large enterprises; it is easier for it than for all others to elect and exercise control over those elected. The Soviet form of organization automatically *helps* to unite all the working and exploited people around their vanguard, the proletariat. The old bourgeois apparatus – the bureaucracy, the privileges of wealth, of bourgeois education, of social connections, etc. (these real privileges are the more varied the more highly bourgeois democracy is developed) – all this disappears under the Soviet form of organization. Freedom of the press ceases to be hypocrisy, because the printing-plants and stocks of paper are taken away from the bourgeoisie. The same thing applies to the best buildings, the palaces, the mansions and manor-houses. Soviet power took thousands upon thousands of these best buildings from the exploiters at one stroke, and in this way made the right of assembly – without which democracy is a fraud – *a million times* more democratic for the people . . .

. . . Proletarian democracy is *a million times* more democratic than any bourgeois democracy; Soviet power is a million times more democratic than the most democratic bourgeois republic.[120]

The danger which faces the new state from the very start is the danger of the restoration of capitalism.

If the exploiters are defeated in one country only – and this, of course, is typical, since a simultaneous revolution in a number of countries is a rare exception – they *still* remain *stronger* than the exploited, for the international connections of the exploiters are enormous . . .

The transition from capitalism to communism takes an entire historical epoch. Until this epoch is over, the exploiters inevitably cherish the hope of restoration, and this *hope* turns into *attempts* at restoration. After their first serious defeat, the overthrown exploiters – who had not expected their overthrow, never believed it possible, never conceded the thought of it – throw themselves with energy grown tenfold, with furious passion and hatred grown a hundredfold, into the battle for the recovery of the 'paradise', of which they were deprived, on behalf of their families, who had been leading such a sweet and easy life and whom now the 'common herd' is condemning to ruin and destitution (or to 'common' labour . . .). In the train of the capitalist exploiters follow the wide sections of the petty bourgeoisie, with regard to whom decades of historical experience of all countries testify that they vacillate and hesitate, one day marching behind the proletariat and the next day taking fright at the difficulties of the revolution; that they become panic-stricken at the first defeat or semi-defeat of the workers, grow nervous, run about aimlessly, snivel, and rush from one camp into the other – just like our Mensheviks and Socialist-Revolutionaries.[121]

Yet, even in the Russia of Lenin's time, these petty-bourgeois masses formed the majority of the population.

Lenin considered the withdrawal of the franchise from the defeated exploiters to be a purely Russian development in a specific situation, not a question of principle for the dictatorship of the proletariat in general. The important thing was that bourgeois democracy was replaced by proletarian democracy. The concept of parliamentary opposition corresponded to a non-revolutionary situation and was meaningless in the context of revolution.

'During revolution we have to deal with a ruthless enemy in civil war; and no reactionary jeremiads of a petty bourgeois who fears such a war, as Kautsky does, will alter the fact.'[122] For that precise reason, the creation of the Soviet state was of international importance.

Bolshevism has popularized throughout the world the idea of the 'dictatorship of the proletariat', has translated these words from the Latin, first into Russian, and then into *all* the languages of the world, and has shown by the example of *Soviet government* that the workers and poor peasants, *even* of a backward country, even with the least experience, education and habits of organization, *have been able* for a whole year, amidst gigantic difficulties and amidst a struggle against the exploiters (who were supported by the bourgeoisie of the *whole* world), to maintain the power of the working people, to create a democracy that is immeasurably higher and broader than all previous democracies in the world, and to *start* the creative work of tens of millions of workers and peasants for the practical construction of socialism.[123]

In the pamphlet from which we have been quoting, Lenin described the Soviet Republic as 'one of the forms' which the dictatorship of the proletariat might assume; in his speech to the Second All-Russia Trade Union Congress (20 January 1919) he spoke of the Soviets – councils elected at the place of production – as *the* international form of the struggle of the proletariat. Their purpose was to produce a new leading class which educated itself though the practice of government. Soviets should give all workers the possibility of direct participation in governing the country and creating a new state order. Lenin considered it an important function of the trade unions to dispel 'the pernicious prejudice that state administration is the preserve of the privileged few, that it is a special art'.[124] Their task was to advance

these millions and tens of millions of working people from simple to higher forms of activity, untiringly drawing new forces from the reserve of working people and advancing them to the most difficult tasks. In this way they will teach more and more people the art of state administration.[125]

Lenin was convinced that the Soviet movement would

spread over the entire world. At the Second Congress of the Communist International he said that the main task of the young Communist parties was to win the masses over to the Soviets.

With the development of Soviet power and the difficulties encountered, Lenin's pronouncements on the dictatorship of the proletariat became less clear-cut. Sometimes he even had to defend himself against the accusation of advocating the use of moral pressure in place of force. He replied that it would be sheer foolishness to suppose that the new science and technology, the construction of a completely new society, could be organized by the use of force alone. The aim was to encourage the masses to cooperate in a willing, disciplined way, to influence the entire population, to persuade bourgeois experts to work for the regime, etc. And at the same time it was necessary to fight bureaucratism. Here a new contradiction, a new but fundamental problem comes into the foreground. In a draft programme of the Party written in the spring of 1919 we read:

The struggle against the bureaucracy, however, is certainly not over in our country. The bureaucracy is trying to regain some of its positions and is taking advantage, on the one hand, of the unsatisfactory cultural level of the masses of the people and, on the other, of the tremendous, almost superhuman war efforts of the most developed section of the urban workers. The continuation of the struggle against the bureaucracy, therefore, is absolutely necessary, is imperative, to ensure the success of future socialist development.

Work in this field is closely connected with the implementation of the chief historical purpose of Soviet power, i.e., to advance towards the final abolition of the state, and should consist of the following. First, every member of a Soviet must, without fail, do a certain job of state administration; secondly, these jobs must be consistently changed so that they embrace all aspects of government, all its branches; and, thirdly, literally all the working population must be drawn into independent participation in state administration by means of a series of gradual measures that are carefully selected and unfailingly implemented.[126]

At the Eighth Party Congress held in March of the same year Lenin said:

We can fight bureaucracy to the bitter end, to a complete victory, only when the whole population participates in the work of government . . . Here we are confronted by a problem which cannot be solved except by prolonged education.[127]

At the First All-Russia Congress on Adult Education held in May 1919 Lenin made the following statement, which somewhat modifies his previous views:

I have shown you that the dictatorship of the proletariat is an inevitable, essential and absolutely indispensable means of emerging from the capitalist system. Dictatorship does not mean only force, although it is impossible without force, but also a form of the organization of labour superior to the preceding form.[128]

The important thing was to win over the middle classes as allies of the movement.

The dictatorship of the proletariat is not the end of class struggle but its continuation in new forms. The dictatorship of the proletariat is class struggle waged by a proletariat that is victorious and has taken political power into its hands against a bourgeoisie that has been defeated but not destroyed, a bourgeoisie that has not vanished, not ceased to offer resistance, but that has intensified its resistance. The dictatorship of the proletariat is a specific form of class alliance between the proletariat, the vanguard of the working people, and the numerous non-proletarian strata of the working people (petty bourgeoisie, small proprietors, the peasantry, the intelligentsia, etc.), or the majority of these strata, an alliance against capital, an alliance whose aim is the complete overthrow of capital, complete suppression of the resistance offered by the bourgeoisie as well as of attempts at restoration on its part, an alliance for the final establishment and consolidation of socialism.[129]

And in his letter of greetings to Hungarian workers, also written in May 1919, he stated quite unequivocally:

But the essence of proletarian dictatorship is not in force alone, or even mainly in force. Its chief feature is the organization and discipline of the advanced contingent of the working people, of their vanguard; of their sole leader, the proletariat . . .

What is needed to enable the proletariat *to lead* the peasants and the petty-bourgeois groups in general is the dictatorship of the proletariat, the rule of one class, its strength of organization and discipline, its centralized power based on all the achievements of the culture, science and technology of capitalism, its proletarian affinity to the mentally less developed working people in the countryside or in petty industry, who are less firm in politics.[130]

When, in the summer of 1919, Russian workers undertook to do a day's voluntary unpaid work on Saturdays, Lenin wrote in *A Great Beginning*:

As I have had occasion to point out more than once, among other occasions in the speech I delivered at a session of the Petrograd Soviet on March 12, the dictatorship of the proletariat is not only the use of force against the exploiters, and not even mainly the use of force. The economic foundation of this use of revolutionary force, the guarantee of its effectiveness and success is the fact that the proletariat represents and creates a higher type of social organization of labour compared with capitalism. This is what is important, this is the source of the strength and the guarantee that the final triumph of communism is inevitable . . .

If we translate the Latin, scientific, historico-philosophical term 'dictatorship of the proletariat' into simpler language, it means just the following:

Only a definite class, namely, the urban workers and the factory, industrial workers in general, is able to lead the whole mass of the working and exploited people in the struggle to throw off the yoke of capital, in actually carrying it out, in the struggle to maintain and consolidate the victory, in the work of creating the new, socialist social system and in the entire struggle for the complete abolition of classes.[131]

Socialism was the first step towards a new form of social labour based on the free and conscious discipline of the workers; in the conscious will to work and to make sacrifices lay the germ of the future society, of Communism.

Communism begins when the *rank-and-file workers* display an enthusiastic concern that is undaunted by arduous toil to increase the productivity of labour, husband *every pool of grain, coal, iron* and other products, which do not accrue to the workers personally or to their 'close' kith and kin, but to their 'distant' kith and kin, i.e., to society as a whole, to tens and hundreds of millions of people united first in one socialist state, and then in a union of Soviet republics.[132]

In later works concerned with the dictatorship of the proletariat the emphasis shifts increasingly to the problem of the alliance between the victorious working class and the working peasants. In the essay *Economics and Politics in the Era of the Dictatorship of the Proletariat*, written at the end of October 1919, we read:

The economic system of Russia in the era of the dictatorship of the proletariat represents the struggle of labour, united on communist principles on the scale of a vast state and making its first steps – the struggle against petty commodity production and against the capitalism which still persists and against that which is newly arising on the basis of petty commodity production.

And further on, spelt out even more clearly:

Socialism means the abolition of classes.

In order to abolish classes it is necessary, first, to overthrow the landowners and capitalists. This part of our task has been accomplished, but it is only a part, and moreover, *not* the most difficult part. In order to abolish classes it is necessary, secondly, to abolish the difference between factory worker and peasant, to make *workers of all of them*. This cannot be done all at once. This task is incomparably more difficult and will of necessity take a long time. It is not a problem that can be solved by overthrowing a class. It can be solved only by the organization and reconstruction of the whole social economy, by a transition from individual, disunited, petty commodity production to large-scale commodity production. This transition must of necessity be extremely protracted. It may only be delayed and complicated by hasty and incautious administrative and legislative measures. It can be accelerated only by affording such assistance to the peasant as will enable him to effect an immense improvement in his whole farming technique, to reform it radically.

In order to solve the second and most difficult part of the problem, the proletariat, after having defeated the bourgeoisie, must unswervingly conduct its policy towards the peasantry along the following fundamental lines. The proletariat must separate, demarcate the working peasant from the peasant owner, the peasant worker from the peasant huckster, the peasant who labours from the peasant who profiteers.

In this demarcation lies the *whole essence* of socialism.[133]

In '*Left-Wing' Communism – An Infantile Disorder*, written in the spring of 1920, one of his most important works to which we shall return later in this book, Lenin tries to arrive at a balanced definition of the dictatorship of the proletariat. He writes:

The dictatorship of the proletariat means a most determined and ruthless war waged by the new class against a *more powerful* enemy, the bourgeoisie, whose resistance is increased *tenfold* by their overthrow (even if only in a single country), and whose power lies, not only in the strength of international capital, the strength and durability of their international connections, but also in the *force of habit*, in the strength of *small-scale production*. Unfortunately, small-scale production is still widespread in the world, and small-scale production *engenders* capitalism and the bourgeoisie continuously, daily, hourly, spontaneously, and on a mass scale. All these reasons make the dictatorship of the proletariat necessary, and victory over the bourgeoisie is impossible without a long, stubborn and desperate life-and-death struggle which calls for tenacity, discipline, and a single and inflexible will.[134]

The full problematic is revealed when Lenin, in the same work, attacks the views of the German Left Oppositionist Communists who, under Rosa Luxemburg's influence, pointed out the danger of confusing the dictatorship of the proletariat with the dictatorship of a party. Politicial parties, Lenin replies, represent class interests and put the most intelligent, influential and experienced persons in the most responsible positions; this elementary truth should be sufficient to dismiss any childish objection. The exploiters had been ousted with comparative ease, but the great task of solving the problem of small commodity producers had not yet been tackled. They could not be ousted; one had to learn to live with them; they had to be transformed and re-educated by means of very prolonged and cautious organizational work. But they corrupted the proletariat and demoralized it with their petty-bourgeois ideas, and that was why the strictest discipline and centralization were necessary within the political party of the proletariat.

The dictatorship of the proletariat means a persistent struggle – bloody and bloodless, violent and peaceful, military and economic, educational and administrative – against the forces and traditions of the old society. The force of habit in millions and tens of millions is a most formidable force. Without a party of iron that has been tempered in the struggle, a party enjoying the confidence of all honest people in the class in question, a party capable of watching and influencing the mood of the masses, such a struggle cannot be waged successfully.[135]

On the other hand, given the special circumstances of a backward country like Russia, was there not a risk that the Party apparatus might take on an independent existence and set itself up in opposition, not only to the working class and the population at large, but even to the Party itself? Lenin himself drew attention again and again to the danger of bureaucratism. In the famous controversy on the role of the trade unions, which shook the Party for more than a year, he tried to give concrete form to his idea of the two aspects of the dictatorship of the proletariat by emphasizing, in contrast to Trotsky, the special function of the trade unions as democratic educational organs.

On the one hand, the trade unions, which take in all industrial workers, are an organization of the ruling, dominant, governing class, which has now set up a dictatorship and is exercising coercion through the state. But it is not a state organization; nor is it one designed for coercion, but for education. It is an organization designed to draw in and to train; it is, in fact, a school: a school of administration, a school of economic management, a school of communism. It is a very unusual type of school, because there are no teachers or pupils; this is an extremely unusual combination of what has necessarily come down to us from capitalism, and what comes from the ranks of the advanced revolutionary detachments, which you might call the revolutionary vanguard of the proletariat.[136]

This function was also necessary because the Soviet state, as Lenin pointed out again and again, was a workers' state with a 'bureaucratic twist to it'.

We have had to mark it with this dismal, shall I say, tag. There you have the reality of the transition. Well, is it right to say that in a state that has taken this shape in practice the trade unions have nothing to protect, or that we can do without them in protecting the material and spiritual interests of the massively organized proletariat?[137]

It will take decades to overcome the evils of bureaucracy. It is a very difficult struggle, and anyone who says we can rid ourselves of bureaucratic practices overnight by adopting anti-bureaucratic platforms is nothing but a quack with a bent for fine words. Bureaucratic excesses must be rectified right away. We must detect and rectify them without calling bad good, or black white. The workers and peasants realize that they have still to learn the art of government, but they are also very well aware that there are bureaucratic excesses, and it is a double fault to refuse to correct them.[138]

In our 1919 Programme we wrote that bureaucratic practices existed. Whoever comes out and demands a stop to bureaucratic practices is a demagogue. When you are called upon to 'put a stop to bureaucratic practices', it is demagogy. It is nonsense. We shall be fighting the evils of bureaucracy for many years to come, and whoever thinks otherwise is playing demagogue and cheating, because overcoming the evils of bureaucracy requires hundreds of measures, wholesale literacy, culture and participation in the activity of the Workers' and Peasants' Inspection.*[139]

The problem of bureaucratism within the state apparatus was, of course, bound up with that of authoritative leadership within the Party, since – entirely in accordance with Lenin's theories – the principal matters of state were decided by the Party. At the Eleventh Congress of the R.C.P. (B.), held in March 1922, Lenin was able to joke about the fact that the intervention of members of the Political Bureau had been necessary in order to decide the fate of a ship with a cargo of tinned food which had arrived at Libau.

But why was it necessary, three years after the revolution, in

* An institution set up to improve the system of control and organization of work in factories and state offices. – *Trans.*

99

the capital of the Soviet Republic, to have two investigations, the intervention of Kamenev and Krasin and the instructions of the Political Bureau to purchase canned goods? What was lacking? Political power? No. The money was forthcoming, so they had economic as well as political power. All the necessary institutions were available. What was lacking, then? Culture. Ninety-nine out of every hundred officials of the Moscow Consumers' Co-operative Society – against whom I have no complaint to make whatever, and whom I regard as excellent Communists – and of the Commissariat of Foreign Trade lack culture. They were unable to approach the matter in a cultured manner.[140]

All Lenin's hopes of overcoming bureaucratism were based upon the raising of the country's cultural level. Did he not, perhaps, overlook certain other important factors? In the immensely important proposals to the Twelfth Party Congress, written on his sickbed a year later, Lenin called for improvements in the administrative machinery, the appointment of a larger number of workers and peasants to the Central Committee, and the reduction of the number of officials on the Workers' and Peasants' Inspection. At the same time he argued in favour of merging the two institutions – that of the Party and that of the state – in order to combat bureaucratism in both. Was not the cure he proposed itself the symptom of a sickness – a sickness which, given the special circumstances of Russia, may have been inevitable, but a sickness which later developed into a chronic disease?

6

STRATEGY AND TACTICS

DEMOCRACY AND SOCIALISM

Lenin never doubted that socialism is the highest, most consistent form of democracy; that the struggle for greater democracy must at the same time be a struggle for socialism; that the main task of the revolutionary working-class movement engaged in the struggle for greater democracy is to find new ways of coming closer to the socialist revolution and, at every stage of the struggle, to win as many allies as possible; that the revolutionary working-class movement differs from the reformist element in the labour movement, not by its contempt for reform, but by its recognition that reforms are a by-product of the revolutionary struggle. So long as the goal of socialism is never abandoned, reforms are to be seen as stages in the struggle.

In *What Is To Be Done?*, Lenin called upon revolutionary socialists to place themselves at the head of the struggle for democracy and to study all questions of democracy with the greatest attention. To believe that this constituted the abandonment of the goal of socialism was to fall into serious error.

... For he is no Social-Democrat who forgets in practice that 'the Communists support every revolutionary movement', that we are obliged for that reason to expound and emphasize *general democratic tasks before the whole people*, without for a moment concealing our socialist convictions. He is no Social-Democrat who forgets in practice his obligation to be *ahead of all* in raising, accentuating, and solving *every* general democratic question.[141]

Convinced that a consistent bourgeois-democratic revolution in Russia could take place only under the leadership of the proletariat, Lenin made this point of view a structural element of his theory concerning the relationship between the bourgeois-democratic and socialist revolutions. In *Two Tactics* he wrote:

Only the proletariat can be a consistent fighter for democracy. It can become a victorious fighter for democracy only if the peasant masses join its revolutionary struggle. If the proletariat is not strong enough for this the bourgeoisie will be at the head of the democratic revolution and will impart an inconsistent and self-seeking nature to it.[142]

He thought, furthermore, that fine distinctions between different forms of democracy should not be ignored. Anyone who overlooked the differences that existed, for example, between Germany and England or between Austria and Switzerland was a very poor Marxist.

In an article written on the occasion of the fiftieth anniversary of the Peasant Reform in Russia (February 1911), Lenin gave concrete form to his views concerning the relationship between reform and revolution within the context of the broader relationship between democracy and socialism. The definition he gave was as follows:

The concept 'reform' is undoubtedly the opposite of the concept 'revolution'. Failure to remember this contrast, failure to remember the line that divides these two concepts, constantly leads to very serious mistakes in all historical discussions. But this contrast is not something absolute, this line is not something dead, but alive and changing, and one must be able to define it in each particular case.[143]

During the First World War, when Lenin was concerned

with the idea of revolution arising from the development of imperialism and the imperialist war, he repeated:

Political changes of a truly democratic nature, and especially political revolutions, can under no circumstances whatsoever either obscure or weaken the slogan of a socialist revolution. On the contrary, they always bring it closer, extend its basis, and draw new sections of the petty bourgeoisie and the semi-proletarian masses into the socialist struggle.[144]

Using the example of national autonomy, which he described as a general democratic problem, Lenin pronounced it a fundamental mistake to believe that a struggle for democratic claims can divert the revolutionary working-class movement from the socialist revolution or relegate the revolution to the background. Just as socialism cannot be victorious unless it achieves complete democracy, so a proletariat which does not wage a consistent struggle for democracy cannot prepare itself for the socialist revolution. On the concrete problem of national autonomy he had this to say:

. . . Autonomy, as a reform, differs in principle from freedom to secede, as a revolutionary measure. This is unquestionable. But as everyone knows, in practice a reform is often merely a step towards revolution.[145]

At the same time Lenin drew a clear line between his own position and that of the reformists, whom he accused of being satisfied with mere reforms and failing to use them as a step towards revolution.

We are by no means opposed to the fight for reforms. And we do not wish to ignore the sad possibility – if the worst comes to the worst – of mankind going through a second imperialist war, if revolution does not come out of the present war, in spite of the numerous outbursts of mass unrest and mass discontent and in spite of our efforts. We favour a programme of reforms directed *also* against the opportunists.[146]

It would be absolutely wrong to believe that immediate struggle for socialist revolution implies that we can, or should, abandon the fight for reforms. Not at all. We cannot know beforehand how soon we shall achieve success, how soon the objective conditions will make the rise of *this* revolution possible. We should support every improvement, every real economic and political improvement in the position of the masses. The difference between us and the reformists ... is not that we oppose reforms while they favour them. Nothing of the kind. They confine themselves to reforms and as a result stoop ... to the role of 'hospital orderly for capitalism'.[147]

Lenin's theoretical views on democracy and socialism on the one hand and reforms and revolution on the other were to assume concrete, practical shape in the proposals he worked out during the period between the February and October Revolutions of 1917. These proposals are perfect examples of Lenin's genius for finding ways of coming closer to the socialist revolution. In *The Impending Catastrophe and How To Combat It* he recommended measures of a revolutionary-democratic nature – measures of nationalization and general democratic control – which would pave the way for socialism.

If we do not employ the phrase 'revolutionary democracy' as a stereotyped ceremonial phrase, as a conventional epithet, but *reflect* on its meaning, we find that to be a democrat means reckoning in reality with the interests of the majority of the people and not the minority, and that to be a revolutionary means destroying everything harmful and obsolete in the most resolute and ruthless manner.[148]

The essence of revolutionary democracy consists in organizing popular control and limiting the power of big capital.

If anything real is to be done bureaucracy must be abandoned for democracy, and in a truly revolutionary way, i.e., war must be declared on the oil barons and shareholders, the confiscation of their property and punishment by imprisonment must be decreed for delaying nationalization of the oil business, for concealing incomes or accounts, for sabotaging production, and for failing to take steps to increase production. The initiative of the workers and other employees must be drawn on; *they* must be immediately summoned to conferences and congresses; a certain proportion of the profits must be assigned to *them*, provided they institute overall control and increase production. Had these revolutionary-democratic steps been taken at once, immediately, in April 1917, Russia, which is one of the richest countries in the world in deposits of liquid fuel, could, using water transport, have done a very great deal during this summer to supply the people with the necessary quantities of fuel.[149]

To carry this through it is necessary to revolutionize democracy, for these measures are a tremendous step towards socialism, a step '. . . from which, if complete democracy is preserved, there can no longer be any retreat back to capitalism, without unparalleled violence being committed against the masses.'[150]

Socialism is the most consistent democracy. Consistent democratic measures, consistent democratic reforms pave the way for socialism. On the eve of the October Revolution Lenin wrote *The State and Revolution*. In it we read:

. . . Democracy, introduced as fully and consistently as is at all conceivable, is transformed from bourgeois into proletarian democracy.[151]

To develop democracy *to the utmost*, to find the *forms* for this development, to test them *by practice*, and so forth – all this is one of the component tasks of the struggle for the social revolution. Taken separately, no kind of democracy will bring socialism. But in actual life democracy will never be 'taken separately'; it will be 'taken together' with other things, it will exert its influence on economic life as well, will stimulate *its* transformation; and in its turn it will be influenced by economic development, and so on. This is the dialectics of living history.[152]

RADICALISM AND SECTARIANISM

Lenin the theoretician was a theoretician of the revolution. Lenin the strategist was a strategist of the revolution. Lenin the tactician was a tactician of the revolution. All his thoughts, his polemics, his actions were placed in the service of the socialist revolution. It is not surprising, therefore, that he was constantly at odds with that current within the working-class movement which was willing to abandon revolutionary perspectives and allow the labour movement to be integrated within the established system, proclaiming – with Bernstein – that 'the goal is nothing, the movement everything' and that the proper aim of working-class struggle is reform on a modest scale. Lenin fought the 'economists' at the turn of the century, the 'liquidators' after the First Russian Revolution, the 'social-chauvinists' during the First World War, and opportunism throughout his life. He never tired of attacking and exposing those politicians and journalists whom he described, in the words of an American labour leader, as 'Labour lieutenants of the capitalist class'. At the same time, however, he felt obliged to make a stand against 'petty-bourgeois revolutionarism'

which smacks of anarchism, or borrows something from the latter and, in all essential matters, does not measure up to the conditions and requirements of a consistently proletarian class struggle . . . easily goes to revolutionary extremes, but is incapable of perseverance, organization, discipline and stead-fastness. A petty bourgeois driven to frenzy by the horrors of capitalism is a social phenomenon which, like anarchism, is characteristic of all capitalist countries. The instability of such revolutionism, its barrenness, and its tendency to turn rapidly into submission, apathy, phantasms, and even a frenzied infatuation with one bourgeois fad or another – all this is common knowledge. However, a theoretical or abstract recognition of these truths does not at all rid revolutionary parties of old errors, which always crop up at unexpected occasions, in somewhat new forms, in a hitherto unfamiliar garb or surroundings, in an unusual – a more or less unusual – situation.[153]

The struggle against left extremism became an important issue in the history of the Bolshevik Party on two occasions: in 1908, in connection with the question whether the Party should take part in the arch-reactionary parliament of the period and exploit the meagre legal possibilities open to it after the defeat of the Revolution of 1905; and ten years later, in 1918, when the Leftists opposed the conclusion of the peace of Brest-Litovsk with Germany. In 1908 the 'Otzovisty'* were expelled from the Party; ten years later the controversy led to a serious party crisis. The central question discussed on both occasions was whether compromises are admissible in principle.

Lenin wrote several articles under the title 'On Compromises'. Over and over again, he used the following example to make his point:

Imagine that your car is held up by armed bandits. You hand them over your money, passport, revolver and car. In return you are rid of the pleasant company of the bandits. That is unquestionably a compromise. '*Do ut des*' (I 'give' you money, fire-arms and a car 'so that you give' me the opportunity to get away from you with a whole skin). It would, however, be difficult to find a sane man who would declare such a compromise to be 'inadmissible on principle', or who would call the compromiser an accomplice of the bandits (even though the bandits might use the car and the fire-arms for further robberies).[154]

The conclusion is clear: to reject compromises 'on principle', to reject the permissibility of compromises in general, no matter of what kind, is childishness, which it is difficult even to consider seriously. A political leader who desires to be useful to the revolutionary proletariat must be able to distinguish *concrete* cases of compromises that are inexcusable and are an expression of opportunism and *treachery*; he must direct all the force of

* From the verb *otozvat*, to recall: those who were against taking part in the *Duma* (parliament). – *Trans.*

criticism, the full intensity of merciless exposure and relentless war, against *these concrete* compromises, and not allow the past masters of 'practical' socialism and the parliamentary Jesuits to dodge and wriggle out of responsibility by means of disquisitions on 'compromises in general' ...

There are different kinds of compromises. One must be able to analyse the situation and the concrete conditions of each compromise, or of each variety of compromise. One must learn to distinguish between a man who has given up his money and fire-arms to bandits so as to lessen the evil they can do and to facilitate their capture and execution, and a man who gives his money and fire-arms to bandits so as to share in the loot. In politics this is by no means always as elementary as it is in this childishly simple example. However, anyone who is out to think up for the workers some kind of recipe that will provide them with cut-and-dried solutions for all contingencies, or promises that the policy of the revolutionary proletariat will never come up against difficult or complex situations, is simply a charlatan.[155]

One of the articles which bear the title *On Compromises* deals with the possibility of peaceful development of the revolution – of revolution without armed insurrection. All Lenin's writings in which this possibility is mentioned date from the very eve of the October Revolution – the first half of September 1917. In this particular article he states his attitude to the question of compromises especially clearly.

The term compromise in politics implies the surrender of certain demands, the renunciation of part of one's demands, by agreement with another party.

The usual idea the man in the street has about the Bolsheviks, an idea encouraged by a press which slanders them, is that the Bolsheviks will never agree to a compromise with anybody.

The idea is flattering to us as the party of the revolutionary proletariat, for it proves that even our enemies are compelled to admit our loyalty to the fundamental principles of socialism and

revolution. Nevertheless, we must say that this idea is wrong. . . .
The task of a truly revolutionary party is not to declare that it is
impossible to renounce all compromises, but to be able, *through
all compromises*, when they are unavoidable, to remain true to its
principles, to its class, to its revolutionary purpose, to its task of
paving the way for revolution and educating the mass of the
people for victory in the revolution.*[156]

The compromise Lenin was proposing here was the seizure
of power by the Soviet and the forming of a government
composed of Socialist-Revolutionaries and Mensheviks. The
Bolsheviks would not demand to participate in this government
but would only ask for complete freedom of propaganda. Such
a compromise would allow the revolution to proceed peacefully and would contribute greatly to the progress of the
international movement for peace and socialism. Disagreements within the working-class movement would be settled
peacefully. By the time the article was published, however,
the possibility of peaceful development had already dis-
appeared.

After the seizure of power by the Bolsheviks, when the
Party was facing gigantic practical problems, when it had to
proceed cautiously while waiting and hoping for revolution
in the West, when it had to enforce organization and discipline
within a war-torn and backward country, the polemic against
'petty-bourgeois revolutionaries' was bound to assume great
importance.

Try to compare with the ordinary everyday concept 'revolutionary' the slogans that follow from the specific conditions of
the present stage, namely, manoeuvre, retreat, wait, build slowly,
ruthlessly tighten up, rigorously discipline, smash laxity. . . .

* The standard (Moscow) translation of Lenin's text here is incorrect.
The passage should read: 'The task . . . is not to proclaim the renounc-
ing of all compromises – which is impossible – but to be able, etc.' –
Trans.

Is it surprising that when certain 'revolutionaries' hear this they are seized with noble indignation and begin to 'thunder' abuse at us for forgetting the traditions of the October Revolution, for compromising with the bourgeois experts, for compromising with the bourgeoisie, for being petty bourgeois, reformists, and so on and so forth?

The misfortune of these sorry 'revolutionaries' is that even those of them who are prompted by the best motives in the world and are absolutely loyal to the cause of socialism fail to understand the particular, and particularly 'unpleasant', condition that a backward country, which has been lacerated by a reactionary and disastrous war and which began the socialist revolution long before the more advanced countries, inevitably has to pass through; they lack stamina in the difficult moments of a difficult transition.[157]

The social origin of such types is the small proprietor, who has been driven to frenzy by the horrors of war, by sudden ruin, by unprecedented torments of famine and devastation, who hysterically rushes about seeking a way out, seeking salvation, places his confidence in the proletariat and supports it one moment and the next gives way to fits of despair. We must clearly understand and firmly remember the fact that socialism cannot be built on such a social basis. The only class that can lead the working and exploited people is the class that unswervingly follows its path without losing courage and without giving way to despair even at the most difficult, arduous and dangerous stages. Hysterical impulses are of no use to us. What we need is the steady advance of the iron battalions of the proletariat.[158]

This social definition of Left extremists, notwithstanding the fact that their critics were also intellectuals, was later to encourage a prejudice against all intellectuals within the Party which continued to invoke Lenin as its leader. It should be borne in mind that Lenin wrote these words in the midst of the crisis provoked by the signing of the peace of Brest-Litovsk, when many intellectuals and students – amongst others –

were vehemently opposed to any compromise with the German power elite and were demanding a revolutionary war for the liberation of mankind. The sharpest lines Lenin wrote on the subject dated from this period (February 1918).

When I said at a Party meeting that the revolutionary phrase about a revolutionary war might ruin our revolution, I was reproached for the sharpness of my polemics. There are, however, moments when a question must be raised sharply and things given their proper names, the danger being that otherwise irreparable harm may be done to the Party and the revolution.

Revolutionary phrase-making, more often than not, is a disease from which revolutionary parties suffer at times when they constitute, directly or indirectly, a combination, alliance or intermingling of proletarian and petty-bourgeois elements, and when the course of revolutionary events is marked by big, rapid zigzags. By revolutionary phrase-making we mean the repetition of revolutionary slogans irrespective of objective circumstances at a given turn in events, in the given state of affairs obtaining at the time. The slogans are superb, alluring, intoxicating, but there are no grounds for them; such is the nature of the revolutionary phrase.[159]

Against the slogans of a revolutionary war, the 'obscene' peace, etc., Lenin set the concrete facts of the masses' desire for peace, the disintegration of the army and the critical situation of the young Soviet state – a situation which the 'disease of revolutionary phrasemongering' could only aggravate.

The times are more difficult. The issue is a million times more important. To fall ill at such a time is to risk ruining the revolution.

We must fight against the revolutionary phrase, we have to fight it, we absolutely must fight it, so that at some future time people will not say of us the bitter truth that 'a revolutionary phrase about revolutionary war ruined the revolution'.[160]

The tone of the article written a day later, to which Lenin gave the title *The Itch*, is even sharper:

The itch is a painful disease. And when people are seized by the itch of revolutionary phrase-making the mere sight of this disease causes intolerable suffering.

Truths that are simple, clear, comprehensible, obvious and apparently indisputable to all who belong to the working people are distorted by those suffering from the above-mentioned kind of itch. Often this distortion arises from the best, the noblest and loftiest impulses, 'merely' owing to a failure to digest well-known theoretical truths or a childishly crude, schoolboyishly slavish repetition of them irrelevantly (people don't know 'what's what'). But the itch does not cease to be harmful on that account.[161]

And after the familiar example of the hold-up to explain the signing of the treaty with the German military leaders, the article concludes:

Ugh! The itch is a nasty disease. And hard is the occupation of a man who has to give a steam bath to those infected with it . . .

P.S. The North Americans in their war of liberation against England at the end of the eighteenth century got help from Spain and France, who were her competitors and just as much colonial robbers as England. It is said that there were 'Left Bolsheviks' to be found who contemplated writing a 'learned work' on the 'dirty deal' of these Americans . . .[162]

On Compromises is likewise the title of an article in which Lenin discusses a remark made to him by George Lansbury to the effect that, since the Bolsheviks were compromising with the capitalists, certain moderate leaders in the British Labour Movement thought that it would be equally legitimate for them to conclude compromises with the capitalists in their own country. Lenin tries to define the essential difference between the two cases as follows:

May an advocate of proletarian revolution conclude compromises with capitalists or with the capitalist class?

This, apparently, is the question underlying the above argument. But to present it in this general way shows either the extreme political inexperience and low level of political consciousness of the questioner, or his chicanery in using a sophism to veil his justification of brigandage, plunder and every other sort of capitalist violence.

Indeed, it would obviously be silly to give a negative reply to this general question. Of course, an advocate of proletarian revolution may conclude compromises or agreements with capitalists. It all depends on *what* kind of agreement is concluded and *under what circumstances*. Here and here alone can and must one look for the difference between an agreement that is legitimate from the angle of the proletarian revolution and one that is treasonable, treacherous (from the same angle) . . .

The idea of compromises must not be renounced. This point is through all the compromises which are sometimes necessarily imposed by force of circumstances upon even the most revolutionary party of even the most revolutionary class, to be able to preserve, strengthen, steel and develop the revolutionary tactics and organization, the revolutionary consciousness, determination and preparedness of the working class and its organized vanguard, the Communist Party.[163]

This article, written in the spring of 1920, also contains the example about the hold-up by armed bandits . . .

When 'Left-Wing Communism' became one of the central problems of the Communist International, Lenin wrote one of his most important works: *'Left-Wing' Communism – An Infantile Disorder*. His aim in writing this book was to give the sister parties the benefit of the Bolsheviks' experience, the international significance of which he emphasized while warning, at the beginning of the book, against the error of exaggerating that significance or extending its scope to include more than the fundamental features of the Russian revolution.

After the victory of the proletarian revolution in at least one of the advanced countries, he wrote, Russia would cease to be the model and would again become a 'backward' country 'in the Soviet and socialist sense'. However, the violent dissensions within the newly founded Communist Parties made it essential to define the ways in which the discipline of the proletariat's revolutionary party is maintained. It is maintained and reinforced in three ways:

First, by the class-consciousness of the proletarian vanguard and by its devotion to the revolution, by its tenacity, self-sacrifice and heroism. Second, by its ability to link up, maintain the closest contact, and – if you wish – merge, in certain measure, with the broadest masses of the working people – primarily with the proletariat, *but also with the non-proletarian* masses of working people. Third, by the correctness of the political leadership exercised by this vanguard, by the correctness of its political strategy and tactics, provided the broad masses have seen, *from their own experience*, that they are correct. Without these conditions, discipline in a revolutionary party really capable of being the party of the advanced class, whose mission it is to overthrow the bourgeoisie and transform the whole of society, cannot be achieved. Without these conditions, all attempts to establish discipline inevitably fall flat and end up in phrase-mongering and clowning. On the other hand, these conditions cannot emerge all at once. They are created only by prolonged effort and hard-won experience. Their creation is facilitated by a correct revolutionary theory, which, in its turn, is not a dogma, but assumes final shape only in close connection with the practical activity of a truly mass and truly revolutionary movement.[164]

One of the lessons to be learned from the mature discipline of a revolutionary party is that of knowing when to retreat.

(We) had to realize – and it is from bitter experience that the revolutionary class learns to realize this – that victory is impossible unless one has learned how to attack and retreat properly.

Of all the defeated opposition and revolutionary parties, the Bolsheviks effected the most orderly retreat, with the least loss to their 'army', with its core best preserved, with the least significant splits (in point of depth and incurability), with the least demoralization, and in the best condition to resume work on the broadest scale and in the most correct and energetic manner. The Bolsheviks achieved this only because they ruthlessly exposed and expelled the revolutionary phrasemongers, those who did not wish to understand that one had to retreat, that one had to know how to retreat, and that one had absolutely to learn how to work legally in the most reactionary of parliaments, in the most reactionary of trade unions, co-operative and insurance societies and similar organizations.[165]

Lenin therefore thought the Bolsheviks justified in basing their attitude to the ideas of the Left-Wing Communists on certain conclusions which they, the Bolsheviks, had arrived at through struggle and sacrifice. For example: should revolutionaries work in trade unions under the leadership of their opponents? The Left-Wing Communists in Germany were of the opinion that they should not.

However firmly the German 'Lefts' may be convinced of the revolutionism of such tactics, the latter are in fact fundamentally wrong, and contain nothing but empty phrases.[166]

We are waging a struggle against the 'labour aristocracy' in the name of the masses of the workers and in order to win them over to our side; we are waging the struggle against the opportunist and social-chauvinist leaders in order to win the working class over to our side. It would be absurd to forget this most elementary and most self-evident truth. Yet it is this very absurdity that the German 'Left' Communists perpetrate when, *because* of the reactionary and counter-revolutionary character of the trade union *top leadership*, they jump to the conclusion that ... we must withdraw from the trade unions, refuse to work in them, and create new and *artificial* forms of labour organization! This is so unpardonable a blunder that it is tantamount to the greatest service Communists could render to the bourgeoisie. Like all the opportunist, social-chauvinist, and Kautskyite trade-union leaders, our Mensheviks are nothing but 'agents of the bourgeoisie in the working-class movement' (as we have always said the Mensheviks are), or 'labour lieutenants of the capitalist class', to use the splendid and profoundly true expression of the followers of Daniel De Leon in America. To refuse to work in the reactionary trade unions means leaving the insufficiently developed or backward masses of workers under the influence of the reactionary leaders, the agents of the bourgeoisie, the labour aristocrats, or 'workers who have become completely bourgeois' (cf. Engels's letter to Marx in 1858 about the British workers).[167]

If you want to help the 'masses' and win the sympathy and support of the 'masses', you should not fear difficulties, or pin-pricks, chicanery, insults and persecution from the 'leaders' (who, being opportunists and social-chauvinists, are in most cases directly or indirectly connected with the bourgeoisie and the police), but must absolutely *work wherever the masses are to be found.* You must be capable of any sacrifice, of overcoming the greatest obstacles, in order to carry on agitation and propaganda systematically, perseveringly, persistently and patiently in those institutions, societies and associations – even the most reactionary – in which proletarian or semi-proletarian masses are to be found. The trade unions and the workers' co-operatives (the latter sometimes, at least) are the very organizations in which the masses are to be found.[168]

Millions of workers in Great Britain, France and Germany are *for the first time* passing from a complete lack of organization to the elementary, lowest, simplest, and (to those still thoroughly imbued with bourgeois-democratic prejudices) most easily comprehensible form of organization, namely, the trade unions; yet the revolutionary but imprudent Left Communists stand by, crying out 'the masses', 'the masses!' but *refusing to work within the trade unions*, on the pretext that they are 'reactionary', and invent a brand-new, immaculate little 'Workers' Union', which is guiltless of bourgeois-democratic prejudices and innocent of craft or narrow-minded craft-union sins, a union which, they claim, will be (!) a broad organization. 'Recognition of the Soviet system and the dictatorship' will be the *only* (!) condition of membership . . .

It would be hard to imagine any greater ineptitude or greater harm to the revolution than that caused by the 'Left' revolutionaries! Why, if we in Russia today, after two and a half years of unprecedented victories over the bourgeoisie of Russia and the Entente, were to make 'recognition of the dictatorship' a condition of trade union membership, we would be doing a very foolish thing, damaging our influence among the masses, and helping the Mensheviks. The task devolving on Communists is to *convince* the backward elements, to work *among* them, and not to *fence themselves off* from them with artificial and childishly 'Left' slogans.[169]

Lenin used similar arguments in dealing with the question of participation in bourgeois parliaments. Some German, Austrian and Dutch Communists opposed this on the grounds that the creation of Soviets rendered parliamentary forms of struggle historically and politically obsolete.

Parliamentarianism has become 'historically obsolete'. That is true in the propaganda sense. However, everybody knows that this is still a far cry from overcoming it in *practice*. Capitalism could have been declared – and with full justice – to be 'historically obsolete' many decades ago, but that does not at all remove the need for a very long and very persistent struggle *on the basis* of capitalism. Parliamentarianism is 'historically obsolete' from the standpoint of *world history*, i.e., the *era* of bourgeois parliamentarianism is over, and the *era* of the proletarian dictatorship has *begun*. That is incontestable. But world history is counted in decades. Ten or twenty years earlier or later makes no difference when measured with the yardstick of world history; from the standpoint of world history it is a trifle that cannot be considered even approximately. But for that very reason, it is a glaring theoretical error to apply the yardstick of world history to practical politics.[170]

It is obvious that the 'Lefts' in Germany have mistaken *their desire*, their politico-ideological attitude, for objective reality. That is a most dangerous mistake for revolutionaries to make. In Russia – where, over a particularly long period and in particularly varied forms, the most brutal and savage yoke of tsarism produced revolutionaries of diverse shades, revolutionaries who displayed amazing devotion, enthusiasm, heroism and will power – in Russia we have observed this mistake of the revolutionaries at very close quarters; we have studied it very attentively and have a first-hand knowledge of it; that is why we can also see it especially clearly in others. Parliamentarianism is of course 'politically obsolete' to the Communists in Germany; but – and that is the whole point – we must *not* regard what is obsolete *to us* as something obsolete *to a class, to the masses*. Here again we find that the 'Lefts' do not know how to reason, do not know how to act as the party of a *class*, as the party of the *masses*. You must not sink to the level of the masses, to the level of the backward strata of the class. That is incontestable. You must tell them the bitter truth. You are in duty bound to call their bourgeois-democratic and parliamentary prejudices what they are – prejudices. But at the same time you must *soberly* follow the *actual* state of the class-consciousness and preparedness of the entire class (not only of its communist vanguard) and of all the *working people* (not only of their advanced elements).[171]

The Bolsheviks had gone so far as to participate in elections to the Constituent Assembly even after they had seized power – because they realized that what is obvious to an avant-garde does not necessarily correspond to the feelings of the masses. In a letter to Austrian Communists written in August of the same year, Lenin explained why he disagreed with their decision to boycott elections to the bourgeois parliament of their country.

As long as we Bolsheviks are unable to take over state power and hold elections, with working people alone voting for *their*

Soviets against the bourgeoisie; as long as the bourgeoisie exercise state power and call upon the different classes of the population to take part in the elections, we are in duty bound to take part in the elections with the purpose of conducting agitation among all working people, not only among proletarians.[172]

Lenin compared the attitude of the 'Lefts' with the manifesto issued in 1874 by a group of Blanquist Communards, declaring that they wanted to attain their goal 'without stopping at intermediate stations, without any compromises, which only postpone the day of victory and prolong the period of slavery'.[173] They imagined that the mere desire to skip the intermediate stations and compromises was sufficient for Communism to be established at once. The realities of the class struggle were very different.

Every proletarian has been through strikes and has experienced 'compromises' with the hated oppressors and exploiters, when the workers have had to return to work either without having achieved anything or else agreeing to only a partial satisfaction of their demands. Every proletarian – as a result of the conditions of the mass struggle and the acute intensification of class antagonisms he lives among – sees the difference between a compromise enforced by objective conditions (such as lack of strike funds, no outside support, starvation and exhaustion) – a compromise which in no way minimizes the revolutionary devotion and readiness to carry on the struggle on the part of the workers who have agreed to such a compromise – and, on the other hand, a compromise by traitors who try to ascribe to objective causes their self-interest (strike-breakers also enter into 'compromises'!), their cowardice, desire to toady to the capitalists, and readiness to yield to intimidation, sometimes to persuasion, sometimes to sops, and sometimes to flattery from the capitalists.[174]

. . . The German Lefts cannot but know that the entire history of Bolshevism, both before and after the October Revolution, is *full* of instances of changes of tack, conciliatory tactics and compromises with other parties, including bourgeois parties![175]

Capitalism would not be capitalism if the proletariat *pur sang* were not surrounded by a large number of exceedingly motley types intermediate between the proletarian and the semi-proletarian (who earns his livelihood in part by the sale of his labour-power), between the semi-proletarian and the small peasant (and petty artisan, handicraft worker and small master in general), between the small peasant and the middle peasant, and so on, and if the proletariat itself were not divided into more developed and less developed strata, if it were not divided according to territorial origin, trade, sometimes according to religion, and so on. From all this follows the necessity, the absolute necessity, for the Communist Party, the vanguard of the proletariat, its class-conscious section, to resort to changes of tack, to conciliation and compromises with the various groups of proletarians, with the various parties of the workers and small masters. It is entirely a matter of *knowing how* to apply these tactics in order to *raise* – not lower – the *general* level of proletarian class-consciousness, revolutionary spirit, and ability to fight and win.[176]

This line of argument leads Lenin to the following definition and conclusion:

The fundamental law of revolution, which has been confirmed by all revolutions and especially by all three Russian revolutions in the twentieth century, is as follows: for a revolution to take place it is not enough for the exploited and oppressed masses to realize the impossibility of living in the old way, and demand changes; for a revolution to take place it is essential that the exploiters should not be able to live and rule in the old way. It is only when the '*lower classes*' *do not want* to live in the old way and the 'upper classes' *cannot carry on in the old way* that the revolution can triumph. This truth can be expressed in other words: revolution is impossible without a nation-wide crisis (affecting both the exploited and the exploiters). It follows that, for a revolution to take place, it is essential, first, that a majority of the workers (or at least a majority of the class-conscious, thinking, and politically active workers) should fully realize that revolution is necessary, and that they should be prepared to die for it; second, that the ruling classes should be going through a governmental crisis, which draws even the most backward masses into politics (symptomatic of any genuine revolution is a rapid, tenfold and even hundredfold increase in the size of the working and oppressed masses – hitherto apathetic – who are capable of waging the political struggle), weakens the government, and makes it possible for the revolutionaries to rapidly overthrow it.[177]

Victory cannot be won with a vanguard alone. To throw only the vanguard into the decisive battle, before the entire class, the broad masses, have taken up a position either of direct support for the vanguard, or at least of sympathetic neutrality towards it and of precluded support for the enemy, would be, not merely foolish, but criminal. Propaganda and agitation are not enough for an entire class, the broad masses of the working people, those oppressed by capital, to take up such a stand. For that, the masses must have their own political experience. Such is the fundamental law of all great revolutions, which has been confirmed with compelling force and vividness, not only in Russia but in Germany as well.[178]

Lenin sometimes saw Left-Wing Communism and opportunism as two sides of the same coin: 'terrorists' and 'economists', 'otzovists' and 'liquidators' alike suffered from a deep-rooted lack of faith in the possibility of winning over the masses for revolutionary action. We read in '*Left-Wing*' *Communism – An Infantile Disorder*:

Right doctrinairism persisted in recognizing only the old forms, and became utterly bankrupt, for it did not notice the new content. Left doctrinairism persists in the unconditional repudiation of certain old forms, failing to see that the new content is forcing its way through all and sundry forms, that it is our duty as Communists to master all forms, to learn how, with the maximum rapidity, to supplement one form with another, to substitute one for another, and to adapt our tactics to any such change that does not come from our class or from our efforts.[179]

You think, my dear oyocottists and anti-parliamentarians, that you are 'terribly revolutionary', but in reality *you are frightened* by the comparatively minor difficulties of the struggle against bourgeois influences within the working-class movement, whereas your victory – i.e., the overthrow of the bourgeoisie and the conquest of political power by the proletariat – will create *these very same* difficulties on a still larger, an infinitely larger scale. Like children, you are frightened by a minor difficulty which confronts you today, but you do not understand that tomorrow, and the day after, you will still have to learn, and learn thoroughly, to overcome the selfsame difficulties, only on an immeasurably greater scale.[180]

At the Third Congress of the Communist International in June 1921 the controversy with Left-Wing Communism came to a head in a debate with members of the Italian Communist Party, founded at the beginning of that year, whose left-wing ideas were summed up in a 'theory of offensive struggle'. Terracini, the representative of the Italian Communists at the Congress, had opposed a resolution which spoke of the need to take over the leadership of the majority of the working class; he had argued in favour of a 'dynamic tendency', a 'transition from passivity to activity', the expulsion of Centrists or disguised Centrists, etc. Lenin retorted somewhat harshly:

If the Congress is not going to wage a vigorous offensive against such errors, against such 'leftist' stupidities, the whole movement is doomed. That is my deep conviction.[181]

I would not altogether deny that a revolution can be started by a very small party and brought to a victorious conclusion. But one must have a knowledge of the methods by which the masses can be won over. . . . Quite a small party is sufficient to lead the masses. At certain times, there is no necessity for big organizations.

But to win, we must have the sympathy of the masses. An absolute majority is not always essential; but what is essential to win and retain power is not only the majority of the working class – I use the term 'working class' in its West-European sense, i.e., in the sense of the industrial proletariat – but also the majority of the working and exploited rural population.[182]

Lenin could not have foreseen that in the developed industrial societies the percentage of the rural population would diminish considerably, while the relative proportion of the new middle classes, and especially of intellectuals, would be appreciably increased. What is perfectly clear, however, is that his advice to Communists was to try to win the sympathies of the masses and convince them of the need for revolutionary development.

THE ART OF TACTICS

Lenin saw tactics as the art whereby the vanguard, with the help of objective facts and of practical experience, can win the masses over to revolutionary action, convince them of the necessity for revolution and persuade them to organize and defend the revolution.

The art of politics (and the Communist's correct understanding of his tasks) consists in correctly gauging the conditions and the moment when the vanguard of the proletariat can successfully assume power, when it is able – during and after the seizure of power – to win adequate support from sufficiently broad strata of the working class and of the non-proletarian working masses, and when it is able thereafter to maintain, consolidate and extend its rule by educating, training and attracting ever broader masses of the working people.[183]

The vanguard could carry out this task only if it was fully

conversant with all the methods and weapons of struggle and was prepared to use any method and any weapon – legal or illegal, parliamentary or extra-parliamentary – without tying itself down to any particular one.

One will readily agree that any army which does not train to use all the weapons, all the means and methods of warfare that the enemy possesses, or may possess, is behaving in an unwise or even criminal manner. This applies to politics even more than it does to the art of war. In politics it is even harder to know in advance which methods of struggle will be applicable and to our advantage in certain future conditions. Unless we learn to apply all the methods of struggle, we may suffer grave and sometimes even decisive defeat, if changes beyond our control in the position of the other classes bring to the forefront a form of activity in which we are especially weak. If, however, we learn to use all the methods of struggle, victory will be certain, because we represent the interests of the really foremost and really revolutionary class, even if circumstances do not permit us to make use of weapons that are most dangerous to the enemy, weapons that deal the swiftest mortal blows. Inexperienced revolutionaries often think that legal methods of struggle are opportunist because, in this field, the bourgeoisie has most frequently deceived and duped the workers (particularly in 'peaceful' and non-revolutionary times), while illegal methods of struggle are revolutionary. That, however, is wrong. The truth is that those parties and leaders are opportunists and traitors to the working class that are unable or unwilling (do not say, 'I can't'; say, 'I shan't') to use illegal methods of struggle in conditions such as those which prevailed, for example, during the imperialist war of 1914–18, when the bourgeoisie of the freest democratic countries most brazenly and brutally deceived the workers, and smothered the truth about the predatory character of the war. But revolutionaries who are incapable of combining illegal forms of struggle with *every* form of legal struggle are poor revolutionaries indeed. It is not difficult to be a revolutionary when revolution has already broken out and is in spate, when all people are joining the revolution just because they are carried away, because it is the vogue, and sometimes even from careerist motives. After the victory, the proletariat has to make most strenuous efforts, even the most painful, so as to 'liberate' itself from such pseudo-revolutionaries. It is far more difficult – and far more precious – to be a revolutionary when the conditions for direct, open, really mass and really revolutionary struggle *do not yet exist*, to be able to champion the interests of the revolution (by propaganda, agitation and organization) in non-revolutionary bodies, and quite often in downright reactionary bodies, in a non-revolutionary situation, among the masses who are incapable of immediately appreciating the need for revolutionary methods of action. To be able to seek, find and correctly determine the specific path or the particular turn of events that will *lead* the masses to the real, decisive and final revolutionary struggle – such is the main objective of communism in Western Europe and in America today.[184]

This task, however, could only be fulfilled if all the existing circumstances, the different pre-conditions and national particularities, were taken into account.

But while the working-class movement is everywhere going through what is actually the same kind of preparatory school for victory over the bourgeoisie, it is achieving that development in its *own way* in each country.[185]

The revolutionary labour movement must not rely on fixed schemes or be tied down to particular forms and formulae. It was the initiative of the masses, their readiness for struggle and sacrifice, their inventive genius which had created the Soviets; the Soviets had never formed part of any previous programme. Marxists should be guided only by certain fundamental lines which might be modified by the experience of the masses.

The crux of the matter lies in political power passing into the hands of the proletariat. When this has taken place, everything that is essential, basic, fundamental in the programme set out in the 242 mandates *will become feasible*. Life will show what modifications it will undergo as it is carried out. This is an issue of secondary importance. We are not doctrinaires. Our theory is a guide to action, not a dogma.

We do not claim that Marx knew or Marxists know the road to socialism down to the last detail. It would be nonsense to claim anything of the kind. What we know is the direction of this road, and the class forces that follow it; the specific, practical details will come to light only through the *experience of the millions* when they take things into their own hands.[186]

The art of tactics is epitomized in the ability to recognize the central problem or task in any given situation.

It is not enough to be revolutionary and an adherent of socialism or a Communist in general. You must be able at each particular moment to find the particular link in the chain which you must grasp with all your might in order to hold the whole chain and to prepare firmly for the transition to the next link; the order of the links, their form, the manner in which they are linked together, the way they differ from each other in the historical chain of events, are not as simple and not as meaningless as those in an ordinary chain made by a smith.[187]

The art of tactics also presupposes readiness to make abrupt changes of policy, to change direction and to explain the necessity for such changes to the masses who are, as a rule, extremely perplexed by them. Two examples of this are particularly worth considering:

(a) the Bolsheviks' attitude towards the Duma (parliament) in the period 1905–8. When, in August 1905, the Tsar announced the convening of a consultative parliament, the Bolsheviks, in contrast to all other opposition parties, decided to boycott it. In effect, this parliament was swept away by the Revolution of 1905. The Bolsheviks maintained the boycott in 1906, a decision which Lenin was later to regard as an error.

What applies to individuals also applies – with necessary modifications – to politics and parties. It is not he who makes no mistakes that is intelligent. There are no such men, nor can there be. It is he whose errors are not very grave and who is able to rectify them easily and quickly that is intelligent.[188]

In 1907 and 1908, when the echoes of the revolution were dying down, Lenin fought the boycott policy. A dozen years later he still thought that

in 1908–14 the Bolsheviks *could not have* preserved (let alone strengthened and developed) the core of the revolutionary party of the proletariat, had they not upheld, in a most strenuous struggle, the viewpoint that it was *obligatory* to combine legal and illegal forms of struggle, and that it was *obligatory* to participate even in a most reactionary parliament and in a number of other institutions hemmed in by reactionary laws (sick benefit societies, etc.).[189]

Lenin's tactics on this question are described in his pamphlet *Against Boycott* (summer 1907). We read there:

The Social-Democrat who takes a Marxist stand draws his conclusions about the boycott not from the degree of reactionariness of one or another institution, but from the existence of those special conditions of struggle that, as the experience of the Russian revolution has now shown, make it possible to apply the specific method known as boycott. ... Unquestionably, a Marxist should make use of representative institutions. Does that imply that a Marxist cannot, under certain conditions, stand for a struggle not within the framework of a given institution but against that institution being brought into existence? No, it does not, because this general argument applies only to those cases where there is no room for a struggle to prevent such an institution from coming into being.*[190]

---

* The second part of this passage being rather unclear in the standard translation, the following alternative reading is suggested:

'A Marxist must make use of representative institutions; no one can

The law of August 1905 had been an attempt to divert the great popular movement from the path of revolution to that of a monarchist constitution; the call to boycott the Duma of 1905 had been a battle-cry for immediate revolution.

As it happens, revolutionary periods are mainly such periods in history when the clash of contending social forces, in a comparatively short space of time, decides the question of the country's choice of a direct or a zigzag path of development for a comparatively very long time. The need for reckoning with the zigzag path does not in the least do away with the fact that Marxists should be able to explain to the masses during the decisive moments of their history that the direct path is preferable, should be able to help the masses in the struggle for the choice of the direct path, to advance slogans for that struggle, and so on. And only hopeless philistines and the most obtuse pedants, after the decisive historical battles which determined the zigzag path instead of the direct one *were over*, could sneer at those who had fought to the end for the direct path . . .

Marxism's attitude towards the zigzag path of history is essentially the same as its attitude towards compromise. Every zigzag turn in history is a compromise, a compromise between the old, which is no longer strong enough to completely negate the new, and the new, which is not yet strong enough to completely overthrow the old. Marxism does not altogether reject compromises. Marxism considers it necessary to make use of them, but that does not in the least prevent Marxism, as a living and operating historical force, from fighting energetically against compromises. Not to understand this seeming contradiction is not to know the rudiments of Marxism.[191]

The autumn of 1905 had been a period of constant revolu-

---

argue with that. But does this mean that a Marxist may not, under certain conditions, fight against the coming into being of an institution rather than fight within the framework of that institution? No, it does not. This general rule applies only when it is not possible to fight against the institution's coming into existence.' – *Trans.*

tionary mass offensives which had successfully harassed the enemy. The slogan of active boycott corresponded perfectly to such a period.

The boycott under such conditions was a natural *supplement* to the electrically charged atmosphere. The slogan did not 'invent' anything at the time, it merely formulated accurately and truly the upswing which was going steadily forward towards a direct assault.[192]

1906 marked the beginning of the revolution's defeat; the Bolsheviks boycotted the Second Duma as well as the first, convinced that this was the best way to fight constitutional illusions among the population. Lenin was later to describe this policy as incorrect. As for the boycott of the Third Duma in 1907, he opposed it energetically from the start.

Boycott *cannot* now have the *same* meaning that it had at the beginning of the Russian revolution. Today we can neither warn the people against constitutional illusions nor fight to prevent the revolution from being turned into the constitutional-monarchist blind alley.[193]

A Marxist is bound to fight for the direct revolutionary path of development when such a fight is prescribed by the objective state of affairs, but this, we repeat, does not mean that we do not have to reckon with the zigzag turn which has in fact already taken definite shape. In this respect the course of the Russian revolution has already become quite definite. At the beginning of the revolution we see a line of short, but extraordinarily broad and amazingly rapid upswing. Next we have a line of extremely slow but steady decline, beginning with the December uprising of 1905. First a period of direct revolutionary struggle by the masses, then a period of monarchist-constitutional turn.[194]

If anyone wants to persuade the *Social-Democratic* proletariat that the slogan of boycott is a correct one, he must not allow himself to be carried away by the mere sound of words that in their time played a great and glorious revolutionary role. He must weigh the objective conditions for applying such a slogan and realize that to launch it assumes indirectly the existence of conditions making for a sweeping, universal, powerful, and rapid revolutionary upswing. But in periods such as we are now living in, in periods of a temporary lull in the revolution, such a condition can in no circumstances be indirectly assumed. It must be directly and distinctly realized and made clear both to oneself and to the whole working class. Otherwise one runs the risk of finding oneself in the position of a person who uses big words without understanding their true meaning or who hesitates to speak plainly and call a spade a spade.[195]

There is no doubt that, in many cases, sympathy for the boycott is created precisely by these praiseworthy efforts of revolutionaries to foster traditions of the finest period of the revolutionary past, to light up the cheerless slough of the drab workaday present by a spark of bold, open, and resolute struggle. But it is just because we cherish this concern for revolutionary traditions that we must vigorously protest against the view that by using one of the slogans of a particular historical period the essential conditions of that period can be restored. It is one thing to preserve the traditions of the revolution, to know how to use them for constant propaganda and agitation and for acquainting the masses with the conditions of a direct and aggressive struggle against the old regime, but quite another thing to repeat a slogan divorced from the sum total of the conditions which gave rise to it and which ensured its success and to apply it to essentially different conditions.[196]

It is not enthusiasm for the *first* 'parliament' that forms a characteristic feature of the moment, not belief in the Duma, but *unbelief in the upswing*.

Under these conditions we shall not be strengthening the movement by prematurely putting forward the boycott slogan, we shall not be paralysing the real obstacles to that movement. Moreover, by doing so we even risk weakening the force of our agitation, for the boycott is a slogan associated with an upswing that has taken definite shape, but the trouble now is that wide circles of the population do not believe in the upswing, do not see its strength.[197]

(b) July 1917. A demonstration led by Bolsheviks was brutally suppressed by troops of the Provisional Government. The Bolsheviks press was banned, a furious campaign was launched against the Bolshevik Party. Lenin, in hiding, wrote a pamphlet entitled *On Slogans*. In it we read·

Too often has it happened that, when history has taken a sharp turn, even progressive parties have for some time been unable to adapt themselves to the new situation and have repeated slogans which had formerly been correct but had now lost all meaning – lost it as 'suddenly' as the sharp turn in history was 'sudden'.

Something of the sort seems likely to recur in connection with the slogan calling for the transfer of all state power to the Soviets. That slogan was correct during a period of our revolution – say, from 27 February to 4 July – that has now passed irrevocably. It has patently ceased to be correct now. Unless this is understood, it is impossible to understand anything of the urgent questions of the day. Every particular slogan must be deduced from the totality of specific features of a definite political situation. And the political situation in Russia now, after 4 July, differs radically from the situation between 27 February and 4 July.[198]

Apparently, not all the supporters of the slogan 'All Power Must be Transferred to the Soviets' have given adequate thought to the fact that it was a slogan for peaceful progress of the revolution – peaceful not only in the sense that nobody, no class, no force of any importance, would then (between 27 February and 4 July) have been able to resist and prevent the transfer of power to the Soviets. That is not all. Peaceful development would then have been possible, even in the sense that the struggle of classes and parties *within* the Soviets could have assumed a most peaceful and painless form, provided full state power had passed to the Soviets in good time.[199]

Now, however, this struggle, the struggle for the timely transfer of power to the Soviets, has ended. A peaceful course of development has become impossible. A non-peaceful and most painful course has begun.

The turning-point of 4 July was precisely a drastic change in the objective situation. The unstable condition of state power has come to an end. At the decisive point, power has passed into the hands of the counter-revolution.[200]

And the political substance is that power can no longer be taken peacefully. It can be obtained only by winning a decisive struggle against those actually in power at the moment, the military gang, the Cavaignacs, who are relying for support on the reactionary troops brought to Petrograd and on the Cadets and monarchists.

The substance of the situation is that these new holders of state power can be defeated only by the revolutionary masses, who, to be brought into motion, must not only be led by the proletariat, but must also turn their backs on the Socialist-Revolutionary and Menshevik parties, which have betrayed the cause of the revolution.[201]

The substitution of the abstract for the concrete is one of the greatest and most dangerous sins in a revolution. The present Soviets have failed, have suffered complete defeat, because they are dominated by the Socialist-Revolutionary and Menshevik parties. At the moment these Soviets are like sheep brought to the slaughterhouse and bleating pitifully under the knife. The Soviets *at present* are powerless and helpless against the triumphant and triumphing counter-revolution. The slogan calling for the transfer of power to the Soviets might be construed as a 'simple' appeal for the transfer of power to the present Soviets, and to say that, to appeal for it, would now mean deceiving the people. Nothing is more dangerous than defeat.

The cycle of development of the class and party struggle in Russia from 27 February to 4 July is complete. A new cycle is beginning, one that involves not the old classes, not the old parties, not the old Soviets, but classes, parties and Soviets rejuvenated in the fire of struggle, tempered, schooled and re-fashioned by the process of the struggle. We must look forward, not backward. We must operate not with the old, but with the new, post-July, class and party categories. We must, at the beginning of the new cycle, proceed from the triumphant bourgeois counter-revolution, which triumphed because the Socialist-Revolutionaries and Mensheviks compromised with it, and which can be defeated only by the revolutionary proletariat. Of course, in this new cycle there will be many and various stages, both before the complete victory of the counter-revolution and the complete defeat (without a struggle) of the Socialist-Revolutionaries and Mensheviks, and before a new upsurge of a new revolution. But it will only be possible to speak of this later, as each of these stages is reached.[202]

Another new phase began when the Kornilov revolt induced the Socialist-Revolutionaries and Mensheviks to seek a rapprochement with the Bolsheviks. This explains why, in some of the articles we have already quoted, written in September 1917, Lenin went back to the possibility of a peaceful development of the revolution, without, however, completely dropping the alternative of armed insurrection.

One of the most important tactical changes in Lenin's career was the swing from 'War Communism' to the 'New Economic Policy', from the Red Guard offensive of the revolution to a policy of careful safeguarding and preservation of the revolution. We shall return to this subject later; for the moment, to conclude the chapter on tactics, let us consider the parable which Brecht found so fascinating. 'Our eyes on the summit, we are happy to walk in the plain,' wrote Goethe in *Wilhelm Meister*. His eyes on the summit, Lenin wrote the following passage to describe revolutionary tactics:

Let us picture to ourselves a man ascending a very high, steep and hitherto unexplored mountain. Let us assume that he has overcome unprecedented difficulties and dangers and has succeeded in reaching a much higher point than any of his predecessors, but still has not reached the summit. He finds himself in a position where it is not only difficult and dangerous to proceed in the direction and along the path he has chosen, but positively impossible. He is forced to turn back, descend, seek another path, longer, perhaps, but one that will enable him to reach the summit. The descent from the height that no one before him has reached, proves, perhaps. to be more dangerous and difficult for our imaginary traveller than the ascent – it is easier to slip; it is not so easy to choose a foothold; there is not that exhilaration that one feels in going upwards, straight to the goal, etc. One has to tie a rope round oneself, spend hours with an alpenstock to cut footholds or a projection to which the rope could be tied firmly; one has to move at a snail's pace, and move downwards, descend, away from the goal; and one does not know where this extremely dangerous and painful descent will end, or whether there is a fairly safe detour by which one can ascend more boldly, more quickly and more directly to the summit.

It would hardly be natural to suppose that a man who had climbed to such an unprecedented height but found himself in such a position did not have his moments of despondency. In all probability these moments would be more numerous, more frequent, and harder to bear if he heard the voices of those below, who, through a telescope and from a safe distance, are watching his dangerous descent, which cannot even be described as ... 'descending with the brakes on'; brakes presuppose a well-designed and tested vehicle, a well-prepared road and previously tested appliances. In this case, however, there is no vehicle, no road, absolutely nothing that had been tested beforehand.

The voices from below ring with malicious joy. They do not conceal it; they chuckle gleefully and shout: 'He'll fall in a minute! Serve him right, the lunatic!' Others try to conceal their malicious glee and behave mostly like Judas Golovlyov.* They moan and raise their eyes to heaven in sorrow, as if to say: 'It grieves us sorely to see our fears justified! But did not we, who have spent all our lives working out a judicious plan for

* The hypocritical and heartless central character of a novel, *The Golovlyov Family*, by Saltykov-Shchedrin. – *Trans.*

scaling this mountain, demand that the ascent be postponed until our plan was complete? And if we so vehemently protested against taking this path, which this lunatic is now abandoning (look, look, he has turned back! He is descending! A single step is taking him hours of preparation! And yet we were roundly abused when time and again we demanded moderation and caution!), if we so fervently censured this lunatic and warned everybody against imitating and helping him, we did so entirely because of our devotion to the great plan to scale this mountain, and in order to prevent this great plan from being generally discredited!'

Happily, in the circumstances we have described, our imaginary traveller cannot hear the voices of these people who are 'true friends' of the idea of ascent; if he did, they would probably nauseate him. And nausea, it is said does not help one to keep a clear head and a firm step, particularly at high altitudes.[203]

7

AFTER THE REVOLUTION

For Lenin, developments after the October Revolution in Russia were always linked with the hope of world revolution which he expected to take place, at first within a relatively short time, later after a certain delay. It was always his conviction that the October Revolution could be finally victorious only when it embraced all, or at least some, of the most important advanced countries.[204] The wave of revolutions in Europe had, as he pointed out, contributed substantially to preventing the Intervention from destroying the young state. The new state had also been aided by the vast size of the country, by the conflicts of the imperialist countries amongst themselves, and, last but not least, by the revolutionary potential of the Russian peasantry.[205]

Lenin had been aware of this potential from an early date, and it was one of the topics on which he disagreed with Trotsky, whom he accused of 'repudiating the role of the peasants'.[206]

The problem of the peasantry, indissociably connected with the fact that the socialist revolution had come about in a country with an overwhelmingly rural population, became crucial after the revolution in face of the country's appalling devastation, famine, fuel shortage, and the grim truth that the socialist revolution in the West was delayed 'for a number of reasons'.[207] A 'respite' was urgently needed to carry out the most elementary reconstruction, to introduce a minimum of accounting and control, and to re-start production.

That is why the present task could not be defined by the simple formula: continue the offensive against capital.[208]

If we decided to continue to expropriate capital at the same rate at which we have been doing it up to now, we should certainly suffer defeat, because our work of organizing proletarian accounting and control has obviously – obviously to every thinking person – *fallen behind* the work of *directly* 'expropriating the expropriators'. If we now concentrate all our effort on the organization of accounting and control, we shall be able to solve this problem, we shall be able to make up for lost time, we shall *completely* win our 'campaign' against capital.[209]

The Red Guard attacks had been necessary because military resistance could only be broken by military means. 'Does that mean that a "Red Guard" attack on capital is *always* appropriate, under *all* circumstances, that we have *no* other means of fighting capital?'[210] The soil had to be ploughed so that capitalism should never again thrive on it in future. But this required other methods. It was necessary to employ bourgeois experts; without their expertise the transition to socialism would be impossible, and it was necessary to pay them very high salaries although this was 'a departure from the principles of the Paris Commune and of every proletarian power, which call for the reduction of all salaries to the level of the wages of the average worker, which urge that careerism be fought not merely in words, but in deeds'.[211] It was necessary to learn, learn, learn; to learn mathematics, administration, economics. The working masses, who had given so many examples of heroism in revolutionary struggle, would prove that in the task of reconstruction, too, they possessed immense reserves of talent.

When a new class comes on to the historical scene as the leader and guide of society, a period of violent 'rocking', shocks, struggle and storm, on the one hand, and a period of uncertain steps, experiments, wavering, hesitation in regard to the selection of new methods corresponding to new objective circumstances, on the other, are inevitable. The moribund feudal nobility avenged themselves on the bourgeoisie which vanquished them and took their place, not only by conspiracies and attempts at rebellion and restoration, but also by pouring ridicule over the lack of skill, the clumsiness and the mistakes of the 'upstarts' and the 'insolent' who dared to take over the 'sacred helm' of state without the centuries of training which the princes, barons, nobles and dignitaries had had; in exactly the same way the Kornilovs and Kerenskys, the Gotzes and Martovs, the whole of that fraternity of heroes of bourgeois swindling or bourgeois scepticism, avenge themselves on the working class of Russia for having had the 'audacity' to take power.

Of course, not weeks, but long months and years are required for a new social class, especially a class which up to now has been oppressed and crushed by poverty and ignorance, to get used to its new position, look around, organize its work, and promote its *own* organizers. It is understandable that the Party which leads the revolutionary proletariat has not been able to acquire the experience and habits of large organizational undertakings embracing millions and tens of millions of citizens; the remoulding of the old, almost exclusively agitational habits is a very lengthy process. But there is nothing impossible in this, and as soon as the necessity for a change is clearly appreciated, as soon as there is firm determination to effect the change and perseverance in pursuing a great and difficult aim, we shall achieve it. There is an enormous amount of organizing talent among the 'people', i.e., among the workers and the peasants who do not exploit the labour of others. Capital crushed these talented people in thousands; it killed their talent and threw them on to the scrap-heap. We are not yet able to find them, encourage them, put them on their feet, promote them. But we shall learn to do so if we set about it with all-out revolutionary enthusiasm, without which there can be no victorious revolutions.

No profound and mighty popular government has ever occurred in history without dirty scum rising to the top, without adventurers and rogues, boasters and ranters attaching themselves to the inexperienced innovators, without absurd muddle and fuss, without individual 'leaders' trying to deal with twenty matters at once and not finishing any of them. Let the lapdogs of bourgeois society, from Belorussov to Martov, squeal and yelp about every extra chip that is sent flying in cutting down the big, old wood. What else are lap-dogs for if not to yelp at the proletarian elephant? Let them yelp. We shall go our way and try as carefully and as patiently as possible to test and discover real organizers, people with sober and practical minds, people who combine loyalty to socialism with the ability without fuss (and in spite of muddle and fuss) to get a large number of people working together steadily and concertedly within the framework of Soviet organization. *Only* such people, after they have been tested a dozen times, by being transferred from the simplest to the more difficult tasks, should be promoted to the responsible posts of leaders of the people's labour, leaders of administration. We have not yet learned to do this, but we shall learn.[212]

The fact that it proclaimed itself a Socialist Soviet Republic was a measure of the Soviet state's determination to achieve the transition to socialism, but it certainly did not mean that the new economic system could already be described as a socialist order. In Russia there still existed patriarchal, i.e., to a considerable extent, natural farming: small commodity production, which included the majority of those peasants who sold their grain: private capitalism: state capitalism in the sense that Russian and foreign capitalists were still active under state control: and, lastly, some socialist production. But the petty-bourgeois element was predominant; the vast mass of peasants who produced commodities inevitably produced capitalism as well. The decisive question facing the revolution, leaving foreign affairs aside, was therefore this:

Either we subordinate the petty bourgeoisie to *our* control and accounting (we can do this if we organize the poor, that is, the majority of the population or the semi-proletarians, around the politically conscious proletarian vanguard), or they will overthrow our workers' power as surely and as inevitably as the revolution was overthrown by the Napoleons and Cavaignacs who sprang from this very soil of petty proprietorship.[213]

The last years of Lenin's life, which coincided with the first years in the life of the new state, were dominated by three major issues, all of which gave rise to impassioned controversy. They were: the peace of Brest-Litovsk, which we shall discuss later; the role of trade unions in the new society; and the 'New Economic Policy' (N.E.P.).

Lenin had always believed that one of the distinguishing features of socialism is the fact that the population is increasingly drawn into the work of administration and government. The trade unions, as a broad mass organization of the working class, had a central role to play in this process.

In this greatest revolution in history, when the proletariat has taken state power into its own hands, all the functions of the trade unions are undergoing a profound change. The trade unions are becoming the chief builders of the new society, for only the millions can build this society. In the era of serfdom these builders numbered hundreds; in the capitalist era the builders of the state numbered thousands and tens of thousands. The socialist revolution can be made only with the active and direct practical participation of tens of millions in state administration. That is our goal but we are not there yet.

The trade unions should know that there is a higher and more important task than those tasks which are partly still in force and partly have already lapsed, and which, at any rate, even if they are still in force, can only be minor ones in our eyes: registration, establishing work standards, amalgamation of organizations. This task is to teach the people the art of administration, not from books, not from lectures or meetings, but from practical experience, so that instead of just the vanguard of the proletariat which has been set to command and organize, more and more fresh blood may enter the departments, and this new section may be reinforced by ten others like it . . .

Their task is to advance these millions and tens of millions of working people from simple to higher forms of activity, untiringly drawing new forces from the reserve of working people and advancing them to the most difficult tasks. In this way they will teach more and more people the art of state administration.[214]

Around the end of 1920 an important and impassioned debate took place concerning the role of the trade unions after the revolution. Trotsky took the view that in a workers' state the workers' special interests no longer needed protection; 'Soviet trade-unionism' should be avoided, and the work of the trade unions should be concentrated on production; the Party should not hesitate to 'shake up' the trade unions in order to create the right atmosphere for production. The 'workers' opposition' used anarcho-syndicalist arguments in support of the principle of direct producers' democracy at the factories. Lenin tried to show that the chief function of the trade unions was educational.

On the one hand, the trade unions, which take in all industrial workers, are an organization of the ruling, dominant, governing class, which has now set up a dictatorship and is exercising coercion through the state. But it is not a state organization; nor is it one designed for coercion, but for education. It is an organization designed to draw in and to train; it is, in fact, a school: a school of administration, a school of economic management, a school of communism . . .

Within the system of the dictatorship of the proletariat, the trade unions stand, if I may say so, between the Party and the government . . .

What are the practical conclusions to be drawn from this peculiar situation? They are . . . that the trade unions are a *link* between the vanguard and the masses, and by their daily work bring conviction to the masses, the masses of the class which alone is capable of taking us from capitalism to communism.[215]

It was necessary, Lenin continued, to face facts, to avoid using military metaphors when discussing the role of the trade unions, and, on the other hand, to take into account the actual level of education of broad masses of the workers.

Does every worker know how to run the state? People working in the practical sphere know that this is not true, that millions of our organized workers are going through what we always said the trade unions were, namely, a school of communism and administration. When they have attended this school for a number of years they will have learned to administer, but the going is slow. We have not even abolished illiteracy. We know that workers in touch with peasants are liable to fall for non-proletarian slogans. How many of the workers have been engaged in government? A few thousand throughout Russia and no more. If we say that it is not the Party but the trade unions that put up the candidates and administrate, it may sound very democratic and might help us to catch a few votes, but not for long. It will be fatal for the dictatorship of the proletariat.[216]

When we read the records of this discussion, which dominated several months of the Party's life, we once more become aware of the principal contradictions in the young Soviet state. Half-way between the position of the administrators and that of the anarcho-syndicalists, Lenin introduced his image of a 'transmission belt' joining the Party and government leadership with the backward masses:

The state is a sphere of coercion. It would be madness to renounce coercion, especially in the epoch of the dictatorship of the proletariat, so that the administrative approach and 'steering' are indispensable. The Party is the leader, the vanguard of the proletariat, which rules directly . . . The trade unions are a reservoir of the state power, a school of communism and a school of management. The specific and cardinal thing in this sphere is *not* administration but the *'ties'* between the central state administration (and, of course, the local as well), the national economy and the broad masses of the working people.[217]

The sailors' revolt in Kronstadt (1921) revealed that the problem of the Party's relationship to the mass of the workers was in fact only one of the many problems facing the victorious vanguard in a country with an overwhelmingly rural population. Most of the mutineers were sons of peasants. Kronstadt contributed to Lenin's recognition that 'War Communism' had become untenable and that new ways had to be sought for securing the country's supplies of food and fuel. At the Tenth Party Congress, which was overshadowed by dissensions within the Party and by the Kronstadt rising, Lenin said:

. . . The conditions in which we have had to defend the revolution made the solution of our problems incredibly difficult. We have not been able to show all the advantages of large-scale production, for it lies in ruins, and is dragging out a miserable existence. It can only be rehabilitated by demanding sacrifices from these very same small farmers. To get industry on its feet you need fuel, you must rely on firewood; and if you rely on firewood, you must look to the peasant and his horse. In conditions of crisis, the fodder shortage and the loss of cattle, the peasant must give his produce on credit to the Soviet power for the sake of a large-scale industry which has not yet given him a thing. That is the economic situation which gives rise to enormous difficulties and demands a deeper analysis of the conditions of transition from war to peace. . . . It is out of such considerations that the Central Committee adopted its decision . . . on the substitution of a tax for surplus food appropriation. . . . We must allow the peasant to have a certain amount of leeway in local trade, and supplant the surplus food appropriation by a tax, to give the small farmer a chance to plan his production and determine its scale in accordance with the tax.[218]

The appropriation of surplus food was replaced by a tax in kind. The country's historical reality claimed its tribute, regardless of the original ideas and illusions of the revolution. Lenin now considered that the victory of the revolution in a backward agricultural country was predicated upon one of two conditions:

In such a country, the socialist revolution can triumph only on two conditions. First, if it is given timely support by a socialist revolution in one or several advanced countries. ... The second condition is agreement between the proleteriat, which is exercising its dictatorship, that is, holds state power, and the majority of the peasant population. Agreement is a very broad concept which includes a whole series of measures and transitions ...

We know that so long as there is no revolution in other countries, only agreement with the peasantry can save the socialist revolution in Russia. ... We must reckon with this, and we are sober enough politicians to say frankly: let us re-examine our policy in regard to the peasantry. The state of affairs that has prevailed so far cannot be continued any longer ...

We must try to satisfy the demands of the peasants who are dissatisfied and disgruntled, and legitimately so, and who cannot be otherwise. We must say to them: 'Yes, this cannot go on any longer'. How is the peasant to be satisfied and what does satisfying him mean? Where is the answer? Naturally it lies in the demands of the peasantry. We know these demands. But we must verify them and examine all that we know of the farmer's economic demands from the standpoint of economic science. If we go into this, we shall see at once that it will take essentially two things to satisfy the small farmer. The first is a certain freedom of exchange, freedom for the small private proprietor, and the second is the need to obtain commodities and products. What indeed would free exchange amount to if there was nothing to exchange, and freedom of trade, if there was nothing to trade with![219]

It seems obvious to us that Lenin not only saw certain fundamental features of the New Economic Policy as necessary in Russia's specific post-revolutionary situation, but also regarded them as basic structural elements of future Socialist states. A letter dated 14 April 1921 addressed to the 'younger' Republics of Transcaucasia is characteristic in this respect. In it we read:

The task is difficult, but fully feasible. The most important thing for its successful fulfilment is that the Communists of the Transcaucasus should be fully alive to the *singularity* of their position, and of the position of their Republics, as distinct from the position of the R.S.F.S.R.; that they should appreciate the need to refrain from copying our tactics, but thoughtfully vary them in adaptation to the differing concrete conditions . . .

You will need to practice more moderation and caution, and show more readiness to make concessions to the petty bourgeoisie, the intelligentsia, and particularly the peasantry . . .

What the Republics of the Caucasus can and must do, as distinct from the R.S.F.S.R., is to effect a slower, more cautious and more systematic transition to socialism . . .

We fought to make the first breach in the wall of world capitalism. The breach has been made . . .

You, Comrades Communists of the Caucasus, have no need to force a breach . . .

Do not copy our tactics, but analyse the reasons for their peculiar features, the conditions that gave rise to them, and their results; go beyond the letter, and apply the spirit, the essence and the lessons of the 1917–21 experience . . .

You must make immediate efforts to improve the condition of the peasant and start on extensive electrification and irrigation projects. What you need most is irrigation, for more than anything else it will revive the area and regenerate it, bury the past and make the transition to socialism more certain.[220]

The critical attitude which Lenin adopted in other writings belonging to the same period towards the phase of 'War

Communism' suggests that the above was not simply an appeal to the Transcaucasian comrades to take due account of the special conditions of their region, but the expression of a more general attitude.

Under this peculiar 'War Communism' we actually took from the peasant all his surpluses – and sometimes even a part of his necessaries – to meet the requirements of the army and sustain the workers. Most of it we took on loan, for paper money. But for that, we would not have beaten the landowners and capitalists in a ruined small-peasant country. The fact that we did (in spite of the help our exploiters got from the most powerful countries of the world) shows not only the miracles of heroism the workers and peasants can perform in the struggle for their emancipation; it also shows that when the Mensheviks, Socialist-Revolutionaries and Kautsky and Co. *blamed* us for this 'War Communism' they were acting as lackeys of the bourgeoisie. We deserve credit for it.

Just how much credit is a fact of equal importance. It was the war and the ruin that forced us into 'War Communism'. It was not, and could not be, a policy that corresponded to the economic tasks of the proletariat. It was a makeshift. The correct policy of the proletariat exercising its dictatorship in a small-peasant country is to obtain grain in exchange for the manufactured goods the peasant needs. That is the only kind of food policy that corresponds to the tasks of the proletariat, and can strengthen the foundations of socialism and lead to its complete victory.

The tax in kind is a transition to this policy.[221]

The time for Red Guard attacks was over; the task now was to learn how to run the country's economy, how to organize production.

We must not be afraid of Communists 'learning' from bourgeois experts, including merchants, petty-capitalist co-operators and capitalists, in the same way as we learned from the military experts, though in a different form. The results of the 'learning' must be tested only by practical experience and by doing things better than the bourgeois experts at your side; try in every way to secure an improvement in agriculture and industry, and to develop exchange between them. Do not grudge them the 'tuition' fee: none will be too high, provided we learn something.[222]

Small peasant farming could not achieve stability without a certain freedom of exchange and without the element of capitalism connected with it; it had to be given this stability, and socialist large-scale industry had to supply it with commodities in exchange for its foodstuffs and raw material. This involved a certain degree of freedom for capitalism, but it was not dangerous because the key positions of industry remained in the hands of the workers' state. Through industry, thus controlled, the backward country could be modernized.

A large-scale machine industry capable of reorganizing agriculture is the only material basis that is possible for socialism. But we cannot confine ourselves to this general thesis. It must be made more concrete. Large-scale industry based on the latest achievements of technology and capable of reorganizing agriculture implies the electrification of the whole country.[223]

'Communism equals Soviets plus electricity': the celebrated formula corresponded to a specific situation in a specific country, but it is far from being universally applicable. Lenin pointed out again and again that N.E.P. represented a retreat, which was in part dictated by the failure of the world revolution to materialize as promptly as expected, and, finally, to materialize at all. At the Third Congress of the Communist International (5 July 1921) he said:

... The development of the international revolution, which we predicted, is proceeding, but not along as straight a line as we had expected. It becomes clear at the first glance that after the conclusion of peace, bad as it was, it proved impossible to call forth revolution in other capitalist countries, although we know that the signs of revolution were very considerable and numerous, in fact, much more considerable and numerous than we thought at the time. . . . What . . . must we do now? We must now thoroughly prepare for revolution and make a deep study of its concrete development in the advanced capitalist countries. This is the first lesson we must draw from the international situation. As for our Russian Republic, we must take advantage of this brief respite in order to adapt our tactics to this zigzag line of history.[224]

It was necessary to face facts.

Our enemy . . . is not the hordes of whiteguards commanded by the landowners and supported by all the Mensheviks and Socialist-Revolutionaries, by the whole international bourgeoisie. He is everyday economics in a small-peasant country with a ruined large-scale industry. He is the petty-bourgeois element which surrounds us like the air, and penetrates deep into the ranks of the proletariat. And the proletariat is declassed, i.e., dislodged from its class groove. The factories and mills are idle – the proletariat is weak, scattered, enfeebled. On the other hand, the petty-bourgeois element within the country is backed by the whole international bourgeoisie, which still retains its power throughout the world.[225]

Borne along on the crest of the wave of enthusiasm, rousing first the political enthusiasm and then the military enthusiasm of the people, we expected to accomplish economic tasks just as great as the political and military tasks we had accomplished by relying directly on this enthusiasm. We expected – or perhaps it would be truer to say that we presumed without having given it adequate consideration – to be able to organize the state production and the state distribution of products on communist lines in a small-peasant country directly as ordered by the proletarian state. Experience has proved that we were wrong . . .

And we, who during these three or four years have learned a little to make abrupt changes of front (when abrupt changes of front are needed), have begun zealously, attentively and sedulously (although still not zealously, attentively and sedulously enough) to learn to make a new change of front, namely, the New Economic Policy. The proletarian state must become a cautious, assiduous and shrewd 'businessman', a punctilious *wholesale merchant* – otherwise it will never succeed in putting this small-peasant country economically on its feet. Under existing conditions, living as we are side by side with the capitalist (for the time being capitalist) West, there is no other way of progressing to communism.[226]

Lenin summed up the whole situation in the famous laconic question: 'who, whom?' Whom would the broad masses of the peasantry follow? The proletariat engaged in building socialist society, which was to supply the countryside with goods produced by socialist large-scale industry, or the capitalists who wanted free exchange and trade as a first step towards the restoration of capitalism? On the answer to this question depended the result of N.E.P. and the fate of Russia's socialist revolution – since the world revolution had failed to take place.

If the retreat turns out to be correct tactics, we must link up with the peasant masses while we are in retreat, and subsequently march forward with them a hundred times more slowly, but firmly and unswervingly, in a way that will always make it apparent to them that we are really marching forward. Then our cause will be absolutely invincible, and no power on earth can vanquish us . . .

Link up with the peasant masses, with the rank-and-file working peasants, and begin to move forward immeasurably, infinitely more slowly than we expected, but in such a way that the entire mass will actually move forward with us. If we do that we shall in time progress much more quickly than we even dream of today. This, in my opinion, is the first fundamental political lesson of the New Economic Policy.[227]

Lenin then asked a few sober and critical questions on behalf of the *muzhik*:

'As people you are splendid, but you cannot cope with the economic task you have undertaken.' This is the simple and withering criticism which the peasantry – and through the peasantry, some sections of workers – levelled at the Communist Party last year. That is why in the N.E.P. question, this old point acquires such significance.

We need a real test. The capitalists are operating alongside us. They are operating like robbers; they make profit; but they know how to do things. But you – you are trying to do it in a new way: you make no profit, your principles are communist, your ideals are splendid; they are written out so beautifully that you seem to be saints, that you should go to heaven while you are still alive. But can you get things done? . . .

If all of us Communists, the responsible officials, clearly realize that we lack the ability to run the economy, that we must learn from the very beginning, then we shall win – that, in my opinion, is the fundamental conclusion that should be drawn.[228]

In the same political report to the Eleventh Party Congress on 27 March 1923 he said that the military battle had been won, but the economic battle still remained to be fought.

The whole point is that the responsible Communists, even the best of them, who are unquestionably honest and loyal, who in the old days suffered penal servitude and did not fear death, do not know how to trade, because they are not businessmen, they have not learnt to trade, do not want to learn and do not understand that they must start learning from the beginning. Communists, revolutionaries who have accomplished the greatest revolution in the world, on whom the eyes of, if not forty pyramids, then, at all events, forty European countries are turned in the hope of emancipation from capitalism, must learn from ordinary salesmen. But these ordinary salesmen have had ten years' warehouse experience and know the business, whereas the responsible Communists and devoted revolutionaries do not know the business, and do not even realize that they do not know it.

And so, comrades, if we do away with at least this elementary ignorance we shall achieve a tremendous victory.[229]

For:

In the sea of people we are after all but a drop in the ocean, and we can administer only when we express correctly what the people are conscious of. Unless we do this the Communist Party will not lead the proletariat, the proletariat will not lead the masses, and the whole machine will collapse.[230]

Lenin regarded the co-operatives as one of the most important links in the chain that would unite large-scale socialist industry with small-scale commodity production. He put forward this view in one of the last articles he was to write before his death:

Indeed, the power of the state over all large-scale means of production, political power in the hands of the proletariat, the alliance of the proletariat with the many millions of small and very small peasants, the assured proletarian leadership of the peasantry, etc. – is this not all that is necessary to build a complete socialist society out of co-operatives, out of co-operatives alone, which we formerly ridiculed as huckstering and which from a certain aspect we have the right to treat as such now, under N.E.P.? Is this not all that is necessary to build a complete socialist society? It is still not the building of socialist society, but it is all that is necessary and sufficient for it.[231]

Strictly speaking, there is '*only*' one thing we have left to do and that is to make our people so 'enlightened' that they understand all the advantages of everybody participating in the work of the co-operatives, and organize this participation. '*Only*' that. There are now no other devices needed to advance to socialism. But to achieve this 'only', there must be a veritable revolution – the entire people must go through a period of cultural development.[232]

Now we are entitled to say that for us the mere growth of co-operation . . . is identical with the growth of socialism, and at the same time we have to admit that there has been a radical modification in our whole outlook on socialism. The radical modification is this: formerly we placed, and had to place, the main emphasis on the political struggle, on revolution, on winning political power, etc. Now the emphasis is changing and shifting to peaceful, organizational, 'cultural' work. I should say that emphasis is shifting to educational work, were it not for our international relations, were it not for the fact that we have to fight for our position on a world scale. If we leave that aside, however, and confine ourselves to internal economic relations, the emphasis in our work is certainly shifting to education.[233]

In his last work, which we have already had occasion to quote – *Better Fewer, But Better* – Lenin spoke of the inevitability of a military clash and once again considered the future of Russia's internal development within the general context of international perspectives.

We, too, lack enough civilization to enable us to pass straight on to socialism, although we do have the political requisites for it. We should adopt the following tactics, or pursue the following policy, to save ourselves.

We must strive to build up a state in which the workers retain the leadership of the peasants, in which they retain the confidence of the peasants, and by exercising the greatest economy remove every trace of extravagance from our social relations.

We must reduce our state apparatus to the utmost degree of economy. We must banish from it all traces of extravagance, of which so much has been left over from tsarist Russia, from its bureaucratic capitalist state machine.

Will not this be a reign of peasant limitations?

No. If we see to it that the working class retains its leadership over the peasantry, we shall be able, by exercising the greatest possible thrift in the economic life of our state, to use every saving we make to develop our large-scale machine industry, to develop electrification, the hydraulic extraction of peat, to complete the Volkhov Power Project, etc.

In this, and in this alone, lies our hope. Only when we have done this shall we, speaking figuratively, be able to change horses, to change from the peasant, muzhik horse of poverty, from the horse of an economy designed for a ruined peasant country, to the horse which the proletariat is seeking and must seek – the horse of large-scale machine industry, of electrification, of the Volkhov Power Station, etc.[234]

Again and again we are confronted with the central problem, that of a victorious revolution in a backward country. In his speech to the Eighth Party Congress in March 1919 Lenin summed up this problem in the following terms:

The result of this low cultural level is that the Soviets, which by virtue of their programme are organs of government *by the working people*, are in fact organs of government *for the working people* by the advanced section of the proletariat, but not by the working people as a whole.[235]

8

ON WAR AND PEACE

Lenin's theory of imperialism was rooted in his conviction that wars are inevitable. The development of the imperialist powers is uneven; in the partitioning of the world, a disproportionately large share goes to the countries which, measured by the rate of development of their productive forces, are no longer in the lead. The resulting conflicts and contradictions have to be fought out by violence.

The question is: what means other than war could there be *under capitalism* to overcome the disparity between the development of productive forces and the accumulation of capital on the one side, and the division of colonies and spheres of influence for finance capital on the other?[236]

Uneven development continually creates situations in which wars become unavoidable.

Peaceful alliances prepare the ground for wars, and in their turn grow out of wars; the one conditions the other, producing alternating forms of peaceful and non-peaceful struggle on *one and the same* basis of imperialist connections and relations within world economics and world politics.[237]

The imperialist powers' partitioning of the world inevitably leads to national wars waged by the colonies and semi-colonies. Since war is the continuation of politics by other means, national wars against imperialism must, of necessity, be the continuation of the politics of national liberation in the colonies.

'National wars against the imperialist powers are not only possible and probable; they are inevitable, *progressive* and *revolutionary*.'[238]

We propose to study Lenin's views on war and peace in three specific contexts: at the outbreak of the First World War, at the time of the signing of the peace treaty of Brest-Litovsk directly after the revolution, and at the moment when the fundamental lines of the Soviet state's subsequent foreign policy were being laid down under Lenin's leadership.

Immediately after the outbreak of the First World War Lenin wrote, invoking the decisions adopted at the last congress of the Socialist International held in Basle in 1912:

The European and world war has the clearly defined character of a bourgeois, imperialist and dynastic war. A struggle for markets and for freedom to loot foreign countries, a striving to suppress the revolutionary movement of the proletariat and democracy in the individual countries, a desire to deceive, dis-unite, and slaughter the proletarians of all countries by setting the wage slaves of one nation against those of another so as to benefit the bourgeoisie – these are the only real content and significance of the war.[239]

Neither of the two belligerent groups of nations is second to the other in cruelty and atrocities in warfare. . . . The follow-ing must now be the slogans of Social-Democracy: . . . all-embracing propaganda, involving the army and the theatre of hostilities as well, for the socialist revolution and the need to use weapons, not against their brothers, the wage slaves in other countries, but against the reactionary and bourgeois govern-ment and parties of all countries . . .[240]

The conversion of the present imperialist war into a civil war is the only correct proletarian slogan.[241]

In all the articles Lenin wrote at the outbreak of the First World War we find violent criticism of the Social-Democratic party leaders who had aligned themselves with their respective

155

belligerent governments. Lenin saw a direct connection between their position and all forms of opportunism within the
working-class movement.

It is perfectly obvious that social-chauvinism's basic ideological and political content fully coincides with the foundations
of opportunism. It is *one and the same* tendency. In the conditions
of the war of 1914–15, opportunism leads to social-chauvinism.
The idea of class collaboration is opportunism's main feature.
The war has brought this idea to its logical conclusion, and has
augmented its usual factors and stimuli with a number of
extraordinary ones; through the operation of special threats and
coercion it has compelled the philistine and disunited masses to
collaborate with the bourgeoisie. This circumstance has naturally multiplied adherents of opportunism and fully explains
why many radicals of yesterday have deserted to that camp.[242]

Revolutionary working-class movements must aim at the
overthrow of their own governments and the transformation
of the war into a civil war. On the eve of the Zimmerwald
Conference, at which 'internationalists' from eleven countries
met in the summer of 1915, Lenin wrote *Socialism and War*.
In it we read:

Socialists have always condemned wars between nations as
barbarous and brutal. Our attitude towards war, however, is
fundamentally different from that of the bourgeois pacifists
(supporters and advocates of peace) and of the anarchists. We
differ from the former in that we understand the inevitable
connection between wars and the class struggle within a country;
we understand that wars cannot be abolished unless classes are
abolished and socialism is created; we also differ in that we
regard civil wars, i.e., wars waged by an oppressed class against
the oppressor class, by slaves against slave-holders, by serfs
against landowners, and by wage-workers against the bourgeoisie,
as fully legitimate, progressive and necessary. We Marxists
differ from both pacifists and anarchists in that we deem it

necessary to study each war historically (from the standpoint of Marx's dialectical materialism) and separately. There have been in the past numerous wars which, despite all the horrors, atrocities, distress and suffering that inevitably accompany all wars, were progressive, i.e., benefited the development of mankind by helping to destroy most harmful and reactionary institutions (e.g., an autocracy or serfdom) and the most barbarous despotisms in Europe (the Turkish and Russian). That is why the features historically specific to the present war must come up for examination.[243]

Not every war has to be condemned; there are also just wars.

For example, if tomorrow, Morocco were to declare war on France, or India on Britain, or Persia or China on Russia, and so on, these would be 'just' and 'defensive' wars, *irrespective* of who would be the first to attack; any socialist would wish the oppressed, dependent and unequal states victory over the oppressor, slave-holding and predatory 'Great' Powers.[244]

Marxism is not pacifism. Of course, the speediest possible termination of the war must be striven for. However, the 'peace' demand acquires a proletarian significance only if a *revolutionary* struggle is called for. Without a series of revolutions, what is called a democratic peace is a philistine Utopia. The purpose of a real programme of actions can be served only by a *Marxist* programme which gives the masses a full and clear explanation of what has taken place, explains what imperialism is and how it should be combated, declares openly that the collapse of the Second International was brought about by opportunism, and openly calls for a Marxist International to be built up without and *against* the opportunists. Only a programme that shows that we have faith in ourselves and in Marxism and that we have proclaimed a life-and-death struggle against opportunism will sooner or later win us the sympathy of the genuinely proletarian masses.[245]

The debate with the 'social-chauvinists' centred particularly on the notion of 'defence of the fatherland'.

What, generally speaking, is 'defence of the fatherland'? Is it a scientific concept relating to economics, politics, etc.? No. It is a much bandied about current expression, sometimes simply a philistine phrase, intended to *justify the war*. Nothing more. Absolutely nothing! The term 'treasonous' can apply only in the sense that the philistine is capable of justifying *any* war by pleading 'we are defending our fatherland', whereas Marxism, which does not degrade itself by stooping to the philistine's level, requires an historical analysis of each war in order to determine whether or not *that particular* war can be considered progressive, whether it serves the interests of democracy and the proletariat and, in *that sense*, is legitimate, just, etc.

The defence of the fatherland slogan is all too often un-conscious philistine justification of war and reveals inability to analyse the meaning and implications of a particular war and see it in historical perspective.

Marxism makes that analysis and says: if the 'substance' of a war is, *for example*, the overthrow of alien oppression (which was *especially* typical of Europe in 1787–1871), then such a war is progressive as far as the oppressed state or nation is concerned. *If*, however, the 'substance' of a war is redivision of colonies, division of booty, plunder of foreign lands (and such is the war of 1914–16), then all talk of defending the fatherland is 'sheer deception of the people'.

How, then, can we disclose and define the 'substance' of a war? War is the continuation of policy. Consequently, we must examine the policy pursued prior to the war, the policy that led to and brought about the war. If it was an imperialist policy, i.e., one designed to safeguard the interests of finance capital and rob and oppress colonies and foreign countries, then the war stemming from that policy is imperialist. If it was a national liberation policy, i.e., one expressive of the mass movement against national oppression, then the war stemming from that policy is a war of national liberation.[246]

As the end of the war drew closer, so the problem of the nature of the peace which would follow it became more acute.

Lenin's position on this question was entirely consistent with his general ideas.

> We are *for* a democratic peace. . . . We shall tell the *truth*, namely, that a democratic peace is impossible unless the revolutionary proletariat of England, France, Germany and Russia overthrows the bourgeois governments.[247]

Two days after the Bolsheviks seized power in Russia, Lenin transmitted his famous wireless message 'To All', in which the Commander-in-Chief of the Russian armed forces was ordered 'immediately and formally to propose an armistice to all the belligerent countries, both Allied and those hostile to us . . . Soldiers, the cause of peace is in your hands! Do not allow the counter-revolutionary generals to frustrate the great cause of peace!'[248] Three weeks later, Lenin drafted the *Outline Programme for Peace Negotiations*.

> The main theme of the political talks and the basic principle shall be: 'No annexations or indemnities' . . .
> Official recognition for each (non-sovereign) nation, which is part of a given belligerent country, of the right to free self-determination, including secession and formation of an independent state . . .
> Withdrawal of troops from the territory seeking self-determination.[249]

The peace negotiations with Germany at Brest-Litovsk led to an ultimatum. Germany demanded that the Soviet state should surrender to Germany all the non-Russian territories occupied by it, as well as paying an enormous indemnity. Lenin came out in favour of accepting these 'annexationist' peace terms, disagreeing with some other members of the leadership who favoured a 'revolutionary' war against German militarism. He argued that the army was already demobilized and the peasantry was not prepared to continue the war; a revolutionary war would be justified only if revolution in Germany broke out within the following two or three months.

If, however, the German revolution does not occur in the next few months, the course of events, if the war is continued, will inevitably be such that grave defeats will compel Russia to conclude an even more disadvantageous separate peace. . . . This being the state of affairs, it would be absolutely impermissible tactics to stake the fate of the socialist revolution, which has already begun in Russia, merely on the chance that the German revolution may begin in the immediate future, within a matter of weeks. Such tactics would be a reckless gamble. We have no right to take such risks . . .

In concluding a separate peace we free ourselves *as much as is possible at the present moment* from both hostile imperialist groups, we take advantage of their mutual enmity and warfare which hamper concerted action on their part against us, and for a certain period have our hands free to advance and to consolidate the socialist revolution. The reorganization of Russia on the basis of the dictatorship of the proletariat, and the nationalization of the banks and large-scale industry, coupled with *exchange of products* in kind between the towns and the small-peasant consumers' societies, is quite feasible economically, provided we are assured a few months in which to work in peace. And such a reorganization will render socialism invincible both in Russia and all over the world, and at the same time will create a solid economic basis for a mighty workers' and peasants' Red Army.[250]

In the discussions which preceded and accompanied the signing of the peace treaty of Brest-Litovsk, Lenin argued again and again that a respite was needed in order to consolidate the gains of the revolution; the interests of world revolution could only be served by saving the revolution in the country in which it had first occurred.

It may be that the respite needed for an upswing of the masses will take no little time, but those who had to live through the long years of revolutionary battles in the period of the upswing of the revolution and the period when the revolution fell into decline, when revolutionary calls to the masses obtained no response from them, know that all the same the revolution arose afresh. Therefore we say: yes, at present the masses are not in a state to wage war, at present every representative of the Soviet government is obliged to tell the people to its face the whole bitter truth. The time of unheard-of hardship and of three years of war and of the desperate disruption left by tsarism will pass away, and the people will recover its strength and find itself capable of resistance. At present the oppressor confronts us; it is best, of course, to answer oppression by a revolutionary war, by an uprising, but, unfortunately, history has shown that it is not always possible to answer oppression by an uprising. But to refrain from an uprising does not mean refraining from the revolution.[251]

Defence of revolutionary war at the present moment is nothing but an empty revolutionary phrase. It is impossible for a ruined peasant country to wage a modern war against advanced imperialism without an army and without the most serious economic preparation. It is beyond all doubt that German imperialism must be resisted, for it will crush us and hold us prisoner. It would, however, be empty talk to demand resistance specifically by means of armed uprising . . .

It is equally empty talk to argue in favour of revolutionary war at this moment on the grounds of support for the international socialist movement. If we make it easier for German imperialism to crush the Soviet Republic by our untimely acceptance of battle, we shall harm and not help the German and international working-class movement and the cause of socialism. We must help . . . the revolutionary internationalists in all countries by all-round, persistent and systematic work; but to undertake the gamble of launching an armed uprising, when it would obviously be a gamble, is unworthy of a Marxist.[252]

The 'left-wingers' within the Party went so far in their

demand for a revolutionary war as to 'accept the possibility of losing Soviet power, which is now becoming purely formal'.[253] Lenin described this attitude as 'strange and monstrous'.

The incorrectness of this view (which was rejected, for example, by a majority of the Petrograd opponents of peace) is as clear as day. A socialist republic surrounded by Imperialist powers could not, from this point of view, conclude any economic treaties, and could not exist at all, without flying to the moon.

Perhaps the authors believe that the interests of the world revolution required that it should be *given a push*, and that such a push can be given only by war, never by peace, which might give the people the impression that imperialism was being 'legitimized'? Such a 'theory' would be completely at variance with Marxism, for Marxism has always been opposed to 'pushing' revolutions, which develop with the growing acuteness of the class antagonisms that engender revolutions. Such a theory would be tantamount to the view that armed uprising is a form of struggle which is obligatory always and under all conditions. Actually, however, the interests of the world revolution demand that Soviet power, having overthrown the bourgeoisie in our country, should *help* that revolution, but that it should choose a *form* of help which is commensurate with its own strength. To help the socialist revolution on an international scale by accepting the possibility of defeat of that revolution in *one's own* country is a view that does not follow even from the 'pushing' theory.[254]

The rejection of the first German ultimatum led to an even more stringent *diktat*, which proved Lenin right. Several times he drew a parallel with the Peace of Tilsit which Prussia had concluded with Napoleon:

We have signed a 'Tilsit' peace. When Napoleon I, in 1807, compelled Prussia to sign the Peace of Tilsit, the conqueror smashed the Germans' entire army, occupied their capital and all their big cities, brought in his own police, compelled the vanquished to supply him, the conqueror, with auxiliary corps for fresh predatory wars, and partitioned Germany, concluding alliances with some German states against others. Nevertheless, the German people survived even *such* a peace, proved able to muster their forces, to rise and to win the right to liberty and independence.

To all those who are able and willing to think, the example of the Peace of Tilsit (which was only one of many harsh and humiliating treaties forced upon the Germans at that period) clearly shows how childishly naive is the idea that under all conditions a harsh peace means the bottomless pit of ruin, while war is the path of valour and salvation. Periods of war teach us that peace has not infrequently in history served as a respite and a means of mustering forces for new battles. The Peace of Tilsit was a supreme humiliation for Germany, but at the same time it marked a turn towards a supreme national resurgence. At that time historical conditions were such that this resurgence could be channelled only in the direction of a *bourgeois* state. At that time, more than a hundred years ago, history was made by handfuls of nobles and a sprinkling of bourgeois intellectuals, while the worker and peasant masses were somnolent and dormant. As a result history at that time could only crawl along at a terribly slow pace.

But now capitalism has raised culture in general, and the culture of the masses in particular, to a much higher level. War has shaken up the masses, its untold horrors and suffering have awakened them. War has given history momentum and it is now flying with locomotive speed. History is now being independently made by millions and tens of millions of people. Capitalism has now matured for socialism.

Consequently, if Russia is now passing – as she undeniably is – from a 'Tilsit' peace to a national resurgence, to a great patriotic war, the outlet for it is not in the direction of a bourgeois state, but in the direction of a world socialist revolution. Since 25 October 1917 we have been defencists. We are for 'defence of the fatherland'; but that patriotic war towards which we are moving is a war for a socialist fatherland, for socialism as a fatherland, for the Soviet Republic as a *contingent* of the world army of socialism.[255]

It is better ... to suffer infinitely greater national and state humiliation and hardships, but to remain at our post as a socialist contingent that has been cut off by the force of events from the ranks of the socialist army and compelled to wait until the socialist revolution in other countries comes to its aid. It comes slowly but it is coming. The war that is now going on in the West is revolutionizing the masses more than before and is bringing near the hour of an uprising.[256]

Lenin's attitude to Brest-Litovsk contains the essential features of his foreign policy during the first years of his leadership of the Soviet state, more especially after the failure of the revolutionary attempts in Europe. They can be summed up as follows: the largest possible number of treaties and agreements; the longest possible period of respite. In a series of replies to questions put to him by a correspondent of the *Chicago Daily News* on 5 October 1919 Lenin explained his position in the following way:

Q. What is the present policy of the Soviet Government on the question of peace?

What, in general outline, are the peace terms put forward by Soviet Russia?

A. Our peace policy is the former, that is, we have accepted the peace proposition of Mr Bullitt. We have never changed our peace conditions (question 2), which are formulated with Mr Bullitt.

We have many times officially proposed peace to the Entente before coming of Mr Bullitt.

Q. Is the Soviet Government prepared to guarantee absolute non-intervention in the internal affairs of foreign states?

A. We are willing to guarantee it.

Q. What is the position of the Soviet Government in respect of an economic understanding with America?

A. We are decidedly for an economic understanding with America – with all countries but especially with America.*[257]

In a draft resolution on foreign policy submitted to the Eighth All-Russia Conference of the R.C.P. (B.) in December 1919 we read:

The Russian Federative Soviet Republic wishes to live in peace with all peoples and devote all its efforts to internal development so as to put production, transport and government affairs in order on the basis of the Soviet system; this has so far been prevented by the intervention of the Entente and the starvation blockade.[258]

This is why Lenin considered the peace treaties with Finland and Estonia as important successes of Soviet foreign policy, designed to frustrate any attempt to turn Russia's small neighbour countries into advance posts for a struggle against the young Soviet Republic. In this connection he described the peace treaty signed between Russia and Estonia as an event of 'epoch-making significance'.

What was it that enabled us to prevail over the combined forces of world imperialism in regard to Estonia, a country which had always suffered violence at the hands of the Russia of the tsars and landowners? It was our proving our ability to renounce, in all sincerity, the use of force at the appropriate moment, in order to change to a peace policy, and so win the sympathy of the bourgeois government of a small country, regardless of all the support given it by international capital . . .

Furthermore, the terms of the peace treaty provide for a number of territorial concessions on our part which do not completely correspond to the strict observance of the principle of self-determination of nations, and prove in practice that the question of frontiers is of secondary importance to us; the question of peaceful relations, however, the question of our ability to await the development of the conditions of life of each

* The English of the replies is Lenin's own. – *Trans.*

nation, is not only an important question of principle, it is also a matter in which we have succeeded in winning the confidence of nations hostile to us.[259]

In a reply to questions put to him by the Berlin correspondent of *Universal Service*, he said:

Do we intend to attack Poland and Rumania?

No. We have declared most emphatically and officially, in the name of the Council of People's Commissars and the All-Russia Central Executive Committee, our peaceful intentions. It is very much to be regretted that the French capitalist government is instigating Poland (and presumably Rumania, too) to attack us. This is even mentioned by a number of American radios from Lyons.

What are our plans in Asia?

They are the same as in Europe: peaceful coexistence with all peoples; with the workers and peasants of all nations awakening to a new life – a life without exploiters, without landowners, without capitalists, without merchants . . .

. . . The basis of peace with America?

Let the American capitalists leave us alone. We shall not touch them. We are even ready to pay them in gold for any machinery, tools, etc., useful to our transport and industries. We are ready to pay not only in gold, but in raw materials too.

. . . The obstacles to such a peace?

None on our part; imperialism on the part of the American (and of any other) capitalists . . .

. . . The influence of peace with Russia upon the economic conditions in Europe?

Exchange of machinery for grain, flax and other raw materials – I ask, can this be disadvantageous for Europe? Clearly, it cannot be anything but beneficial . . .

Is Russia ready to enter into business relations with America?

Of course she is ready to do so, and with all countries. Peace with Estonia, to whom we have conceded a great deal, has proved our readiness, for the sake of business relations, to give even industrial concessions on certain conditions.[260]

At the same time Lenin remained faithful to the idea that wars under imperialism are unavoidable and that an eventual attack on the Soviet Union was to be expected. At the Ninth Party Congress in March 1920 he stated:

But the measures we take for peace must be accompanied by intensified preparedness for defence, and in no case must our army be disarmed. Our army offers a real guarantee that the imperialist powers will not make the slightest attempt or encroachment on us; for although they might count on certain ephemeral successes at first, not one of them would escape defeat at the hands of Soviet Russia. That we must realize, that must be made the basis of our agitation and propaganda, that is what we must prepare for, in order to solve the problem which, in view of our growing fatigue, compels us to combine the one with the other.[261]

The attempt of world imperialism to crush us by military force has collapsed completely. The international situation has now given us a much longer and more durable respite than the one we had at the beginning of the revolution. But we must remember that this is nothing more than a respite. We must remember that the whole capitalist world is armed to the teeth and is only waiting for the moment, choosing the best strategical conditions, and studying the means of attack. We must never under any circumstances forget that all the economic power and all the military power is still on its side.[262]

Eight months later, when the attempts at intervention had been successfully repulsed, Lenin spoke of a time gain which was far more important than a mere breathing-space.

Thus a glance at our international position as a whole will show that we have achieved tremendous successes and have won, not only a breathing-space, but something much more significant. By a breathing-space we understand a brief period during which the imperialist powers have had many opportunities to renew in greater force the war against us. Today, too, we do not underestimate the danger and do not deny the possibility of future military intervention by the capitalist countries. It is essential for us to maintain our military preparedness. However, if we cast a glance at the conditions in which we defeated all attempts made by the Russian counter-revolutionaries and achieved a formal peace with all the Western states, it will be clear that we have something more than a breathing-space: we have entered a new period, in which we have won the right to our fundamental international existence in the network of capitalist states.[263]

In this situation the important thing was to exploit the differences among the capitalist states in the interests of the Soviet Union's own security.

While we stand alone and the capitalist world is strong, our foreign policy consists ... in our having to utilize disagreements (to vanquish all the imperialist powers would, of course, be a most pleasant thing, but for a fairly long time we shall not be in a position to do so).[264]

A Russian delegation took part in the international economic conference held in Genoa in the spring of 1922 This conference was followed by the Rapallo Conference, at which the definitive peace treaty with Germany was signed. On this issue Lenin said:

From the very beginning we declared that *we welcomed Genoa and would attend it*. We understood perfectly well and did not in the least conceal the fact that we were going there as merchants, because trade with capitalist countries (as long as they have not entirely collapsed) is absolutely essential to us; we realized that we were going to Genoa to bargain for the most proper and most advantageous and politically suitable terms for this trade, and nothing more. This is by no means a secret to those capitalist countries whose governments drew up the first place for the Genoa Conference and got it going. Those countries know perfectly well that the list of commercial agreements linking us with different capitalist states is growing longer and longer, that the number of practical transactions is increasing, and that we are now discussing in the greatest detail a huge number of joint Russian and foreign commercial projects between the most diverse combinations of foreign countries and various branches of our industry. Thus, the capitalist states are well aware of the practical basis of what is mainly to be discussed at Genoa.[265]

In the same speech he quoted approvingly the following order of the day issued to the Red Army by Trotsky:

'Let every man of the Red Army get a clear understanding of the international situation. We know definitely that there is a permanent group over there who want to try their hand at intervention. We shall be on the alert. Let every man of the Red Army know all about the diplomatic game and what is meant by force of arms, which, up to now, has decided all class conflicts.'[266]

In a draft decision of the All-Russia Central Executive Committee on the report of the delegation to the Genoa Conference, Lenin gave a general definition of Soviet policy. He spoke of the 'equality of the two property systems' (capitalist or private property and communist property, at that time established only in the R.S.F.S.R.),* which indirectly meant 'the collapse, the bankruptcy of the first property system and the inevitability of its coming to an agreement with the second, on terms of equality'.

True equality of the two property systems – *if only as a temporary state, until such time as the entire world abandons* private property and the economic chaos and wars engendered by it for the higher property system – is found only in the Treaty of Rapallo.[267]

What, then, was the fundamental principle of Lenin's

* Russian Soviet Federative Socialist Republic, the first republic of the Soviet Union. – *Trans.*

foreign policy? It amounts to this: in a world which is not yet socialist, where different property systems coexist and where wars and attacks on the Soviet state have to be reckoned with, it is necessary to pursue a policy of peaceful agreements. When the International Federation of Trade Unions convened an international peace congress at The Hague in December 1922, Lenin said that the most important task of the Soviet delegation to the congress was to

explain the real situation to the people, show them that war is hatched in the greatest secrecy, and that the ordinary workers' organizations, even if they call themselves revolutionary organizations, are utterly helpless in face of a really impending war.

We must explain to the people again and again in the most concrete manner possible how matters stood in the last war, and why they could not have been otherwise.[268]

In his last published work, *Better Fewer, But Better*, which we have repeatedly quoted before, Lenin again spoke of the inevitability of wars and military conflicts 'between the counter-revolutionary imperialist West and the revolutionary and nationalist East'.[269] The later claim that Lenin's views on Soviet foreign policy were a kind of certificate of legitimacy for the policy of peaceful coexistence inaugurated by Khrushchev lacks any sound factual basis.

9

LENINISM

Immediately after Lenin's death, Stalin defined Leninism as 'Marxism in the epoch of imperialism and proletarian revolutions', and presented Lenin's ideas as the only interpretation of scientific socialism valid in our time, virtually canonizing his views on all questions and in all fields. As a result, quotations from Lenin, all too often taken out of context, assumed the weight of final and definitive arguments on all subjects. This was at variance, not only with the critical spirit of Marxism, but also with the spirit of Lenin himself. Bertrand Russell wrote after visiting Moscow that he had never met an important person so utterly devoid of a sense of his own importance as Lenin. Modesty and the rejection of any kind of personality cult were characteristic of him throughout his life. He was quite content with a flat occupying an area of twenty-six square metres in the Kremlin, the meals he ate were collected by his wife from a nearby restaurant, he avoided all luxury, and when the Ninth Party Congress was about to celebrate his fiftieth birthday, he actually ran away.

Without attempting to analyse the uses and abuses of Lenin quotations, we should mention in passing that many of his pronouncements – such as, for example, his diatribes against bureaucratism and Great-Russian chauvinism, or his attacks on 'komchvanstvo' (communist arrogance) – were conveniently forgotten with quite remarkable speed. It would have been too much to expect that the following passage from his celebrated lecture on the Revolution of 1905 might have been quoted in his homeland on the occasion of the centenary of his birth:

Tsarism vented its hatred particularly upon the Jews. On the one hand, the Jews furnished a particularly high percentage (compared with the total Jewish population) of leaders of the revolutionary movement. And now, too, it should be noted to the credit of the Jews, they furnish a relatively high percentage of internationalists, compared with other nations. On the other hand, tsarism adroitly exploited the basest anti-Jewish prejudices of the most ignorant strata of the population in order to organize, if not to lead directly, pogroms – over 4,000 were killed and more than 10,000 mutilated in 100 towns. These atrocious massacres of peaceful Jews, their wives and children, roused disgust throughout the civilized world.[270]

The selective canonization of Lenin's views has led to a situation in which opinions on matters in which he was not necessarily at his strongest are presented as binding and obligatory for all Marxists. This applies, in particular, to the sphere of philosophy. Lenin never considered himself a great philosopher; his book *Materialism and Empirio-Criticism* was written in 1908 as part of a political controversy with the Machist and positivist views of a group within the Party with which he was in disagreement on political grounds as well. 'It is *hellishly* important to me', he wrote in a letter to his sister at that time, 'for the book to appear sooner. I have not only literary but also serious political commitments that are linked up with the publication of the book.'[271]

Using Engels's *Anti-Dühring* as his starting point and treating Marxism not only as a method of studying social phenomena and a scientific methodology of historical action, but also as a scientific world view, Lenin attempted to apply Engels's fundamental ideas to the specific ideological debate set off by the latest discoveries in the natural sciences. His principal aim was to interpret the controversy between Marxism and idealism as the expression of the class struggle – indeed, to interpret the entire history of philosophy as a struggle between the attitudes adopted by Plato and Democritus respectively.

He argued, with Engels, that the difference between the materialists and the idealists consists in the fact that the materialists take nature to be primary and the mind secondary, whereas the opposite is true of the idealists.

Materialism, in full agreement with natural science, takes matter as primary and regards consciousness, thought, sensation as secondary, because in its well-defined form sensation is associated only with the higher forms of matter (organic matter), while 'in the foundation of the structure of matter' one can only surmise the existence of a faculty akin to sensation.[272]

The same *experience* (not in the Machist sense, but in the human sense of the term) that has produced in us the firm conviction that *independently* of us there exist other people, and not mere complexes of my sensations of high, short, yellow, hard, etc. – this same *experience* produces in us the conviction that things, the world, the environment exist independently of us. Our sensation, our consciousness is only *an image* of the external world, and it is obvious that an image cannot exist without the thing imaged, and that the latter exists independently of that which images it.[273]

Nature existed before man; the earth was formed before any human consciousness could perceive it. The two basic directions in philosophy give rise to the two basic directions in epistemology. Matter is the philosophical category for the existence of the outside world; but the idealists, in essence, still believe with Bishop Berkeley that things exist only in the consciousness of man. The most effective refutation of this school of thought is the criterion of practice.

The existence of the thing reflected independent of the reflector (the independence of the external world from the mind) is the fundamental tenet of materialism.[274]

Matter is a philosophical category denoting the objective reality which is given to man by his sensations, and which is copied, photographed and reflected by our sensations, while existing independently of them. Therefore, to say that such a concept can become 'antiquated' is *childish talk,* a senseless repetition of the arguments of fashionable *reactionary* philosophy. Could the struggle between materialism and idealism, the struggle between the tendencies or lines of Plato and Democritus in philosophy, the struggle between religion and science, the denial of objective truth and its assertion, the struggle between the adherents of supersensible knowledge and its adversaries, have become antiquated during the two thousand years of the development of philosophy?[275]

There is an objective truth, to which we come increasingly closer through an endless process of thought by way of relative truths.

Dialectics – as Hegel in his time explained – *contains* an element of relativism, of negation, of scepticism, but *is not reducible* to relativism. The materialist dialectics of Marx and Engels certainly does contain relativism, but is not reducible to relativism, that is, it recognizes the relativity of all our knowledge, not in the sense of denying objective truth, but in the sense that the limits of approximation of our knowledge to this truth are historically conditional.[276]

With Engels, Lenin draws a distinction between dialectical and mechanical materialism:

It is mainly because the physicists did not know dialectics that the new physics strayed into idealism. They combated metaphysical (in Engels's, and not the positivist, i.e., Humean, sense of the word) materialism and its one-sided 'mechanism', and in so doing threw out the baby with the bath-water. Denying the immutability of the elements and of the properties of matter known hitherto, they ended by denying matter, i.e., the objective reality of the physical world. Denying the absolute character of some of the most important and basic laws, they ended by denying all objective law in nature and by declaring that a law of nature is a mere convention, 'a limitation of expectation', 'a logical necessity', and so forth. Insisting on the approximate and relative character of our knowledge, they ended by denying the object independent of the mind, reflected approximately-correctly and relatively-truthfully by the mind. And so on, and so forth, without end.[277]

And he sums up:

Materialism in general recognizes objectively real being (matter) as independent of the consciousness, sensation, experience, etc., of humanity. Historical materialism recognizes social being as independent of the social consciousness of humanity. In both cases consciousness is only the reflection of being, at best an approximately true (adequate, perfectly exact) reflection of it. From this Marxist philosophy, which is cast from a single piece of steel, you cannot eliminate one basic premise, one essential part, without departing from objective truth, without falling prey to bourgeois-reactionary falsehood.[278]

The controversy between materialism and idealism is the philosophical expression of class antagonism. Positivism is 'total reaction'. All it does is to disguise the old philosophy of idealism with a new phraseology. Behind the epistemological scholasticism of empirio-criticism

one must not fail to see the struggle of parties in philosophy, a struggle which in the last analysis reflects the tendencies and ideology of the antagonistic classes in modern society. Recent philosophy is as partisan as was philosophy two thousand years ago. The contending parties are essentially – although this is concealed by a pseudo-erudite quackery of new terms or by a weak-minded non-partisanship – materialism and idealism. The latter is merely a subtle, refined form of fideism, which stands fully armed, commands vast organizations and steadily continues to exercise influence on the masses, turning the slightest vacillation in philosophical thought to its own advantage. The objective, class role of empirio-criticism consists entirely in rendering faithful service to the fideists in their struggle against materialism in general and historical materialism in particular.[279]

Materialism and Empirio-Criticism has been treated as though it were *the* standard work on dialectical materialism and Marxist philosophy. Yet it is not the only work in which Lenin expressed himself on philosophical matters. In a series of notes, fragments and abstracts written chiefly in the years 1914 and 1915, we find ideas which are considerably more subtle than those embodied in *Materialism and Empirio-Criticism*.

In a conspectus of Hegel's *Science of Logic*:

Not only Wesen (essence) but Schein (semblance), too, is objective. There is a difference between the subjective and the objective, BUT IT, TOO, HAS ITS LIMITS.[280]

In these notes, Lenin's judgement of philosophical systems is no longer a matter of simple polarities, as it had been in 1908.

In general, the refutation of a philosophic system does not mean discarding it, but developing it further, not replacing it by another, one-sided opposed system, but incorporating it into something more advanced.[281]

The impact of Hegel produces the following aphorism:

It is impossible completely to understand Marx's *Capital*, and especially its first chapter, without having thoroughly studied and understood the *whole* of Hegel's *Logic*. Consequently, half a century later none of the Marxists understood Marx![282]

The definition of cognition as the reflection of reality is seen less crudely than before:

Logic is the science of cognition. It is the theory of knowledge. Knowledge is the reflection of nature by man. But this is not a simple, not an immediate, not a complete reflection, but the process of a series of abstractions, the formation and development of concepts, laws, etc., and these concepts, laws, etc. (thought, science = 'the logical Idea') *embrace* conditionally, approximately, the universal law-governed character of eternally moving and developing nature. Here there are *actually*, objectively, *three* members: (1) nature; (2) human cognition = the human *brain* (as the highest product of this same nature), and (3) the form of reflection of nature in human cognition, and this form consists precisely of concepts, laws, categories, etc. Man cannot comprehend = reflect = mirror nature *as a whole*, in its completeness, its 'immediate totality', he can only *eternally* come closer to this, creating abstractions, concepts, laws, a scientific picture of the world, etc., etc.[283]

The coincidence of thought with the object is a *process*: thought (= man) must not imagine truth in the form of dead repose, in the form of a bare picture (image), pale (matt), without impulse, without motion, like a genius, like a number, like abstract thought.[284]

He no longer evaluates philosophical systems on the basis of class associations. In a conspectus of Hegel's *Lectures on the History of Philosophy* we read:

Intelligent idealism is closer to intelligent materialism than stupid materialism.

Dialectical idealism instead of intelligent; metaphysical, underdeveloped, dead, crude, rigid instead of stupid.[285]

Hegel seriously 'believed', thought, that materialism as a philosophy was impossible, for philosophy is the science of thinking, of the *universal*, but the universal is a thought. Here he repeated the error of the same subjective idealism that he always called 'bad' idealism. Objective (and still more, absolute) idealism came *very close* to materialism by a zig-zag (and a somersault), even partially *became transformed into it*.[286]

And in a note on the question of dialectics, Lenin says:

Philosophical idealism is *only* nonsense from the standpoint of crude, simple, metaphysical materialism. From the standpoint of *dialectical* materialism, on the other hand, philosophical idealism is a *one-sided*, exaggerated, *überschwengliches*** (Dietzgen) development (inflation, distention) of one of the features, aspects, facets of knowledge into an absolute, *divorced* from matter, from nature, apotheosized.[287]

There is not a single line in any article or speech by Lenin to suggest that he ever regarded himself as the only interpreter of scientific socialism or as an infallible Marxist authority in all spheres and on all questions.

The attempt to manufacture a 'Marxist-Leninist aesthetic' out of a few scattered remarks is even less convincing.

Lenin, the great revolutionary, had conservative tastes in literature and art. He loved Pushkin, admired Tolstoy, and was puzzled by Mayakovsky (although he conceded that, if the revolutionary young were enthusiastic about Mayakovsky's poetry, there must be something in it). He never elevated his personal taste to the status of an aesthetic law and never claimed to be the Party's *ex officio* spokesman on literature and art.

His cruder followers have turned him, posthumously and quite without justification, into the inventor of a new aesthetic category – the category of 'party-mindedness'. The text they generally invoke is an article entitled *Party Organization and Party Literature*, published on 26 November 1906.

So long as there was a distinction between the illegal and the legal press, the question of the party and non-party press was decided extremely simply and in an extremely false and abnormal way. The entire illegal press was a party press, being published by organizations and run by groups which in one way or another were linked with groups of practical party workers. The entire

* Extravagant. – *Trans.*

legal press was non-party – since parties were banned – but it 'gravitated' towards one party or another. Unnatural alliances, strange 'bed-fellows' and false cover-devices were inevitable. The forced reserve of those who wished to express party views merged with the immature thinking or mental cowardice of those who had not risen to these views and who were not, in effect, party people.

An accursed period of Aesopian language, literary bondage, slavish speech, and ideological serfdom! The proletariat has put an end to this foul atmosphere which stifled everything living and fresh in Russia. But so far the proletariat has won only half freedom for Russia.[288]

The incomplete revolution, characterized by an unnatural combination of open, consistent and forthright party views with an underground, covert, 'diplomatic', dodgy 'legality', compelled the Party to demand an open declaration of allegiance from those journalists and writers who belonged to it. Literature had to become Party literature.

Literature must become *part* of the common cause of the proletariat, 'a cog and a screw' of one single great Social-Democratic mechanism set in motion by the entire politically-conscious vanguard of the entire working class. Literature must become a component of organized, planned and integrated Social-Democratic Party work.[289]

But Lenin was critical of his own exaggerated formulation.

'All comparisons are lame,' says a German proverb. So is my comparison of literature with a cog, of a living movement with a mechanism. And I daresay there will ever be hysterical intellectuals to raise a howl about such a comparison, which degrades, deadens, 'bureaucratizes' the free battle of ideas, freedom of criticism, freedom of literary creation, etc., etc. Such outcries, in point of fact, would be nothing more than an expression of bourgeois-intellectual individualism. There is no question that literature is least of all subject to mechanical adjustment or levelling, to the rule of the majority over the minority. There is no question, either, that in this field greater scope must undoubtedly be allowed for personal initiative, individual inclination, thought and fantasy, form and content. All this is undeniable; but all this simply shows that the literary side of the proletarian party cause cannot be mechanically identified with its other sides. This, however, does not in the least refute the proposition, alien and strange to the bourgeoisie and bourgeois democracy, that literature must by all means and necessarily become an element of Social-Democratic Party work, inseparably bound up with the other elements.[290]

What he meant was not literature in general but 'the literary part of party activity' – Party literature and political journalism. He demanded that:

Newspapers must become the organs of the various party organizations, and their writers must by all means become members of these organizations. Publishing and distributing centres, bookshops and reading-rooms, libraries and similar establishments must all be under party control.[290]

Anticipating the objection that he wanted ordinary workers to decide questions of science, philosophy or aesthetics, by a show of hands, Lenin retorted:

Calm yourselves, gentlemen! First of all, we are discussing party literature and its subordination to party control. Everyone is free to write and say whatever he likes, without any restrictions. But every voluntary association (including a party) is also free to expel members who use the name of the party to advocate anti-Party views. Freedom of speech and the press must be complete. But then freedom of association must be complete too. I am bound to accord you, in the name of free speech, the full right to shout, lie and write to your heart's content. But you are bound to grant me, in the name of freedom of association, the right to enter into, or withdraw from, association with people advocating this or that view. The Party is a voluntary association, which would inevitably break up, first ideologically and then physically, if it did not cleanse itself of people advocating anti-party views. . . . Freedom of thought and freedom of criticism within the Party will never make us forget about the freedom of organizing people into those voluntary associations known as parties.[291]

This presupposes a situation in which political parties are voluntary associations, membership of which does not entail any advantages and expulsion no disadvantages. Whoever joins a party of his own free will may not speak or write against the party. But within the party he is guaranteed full freedom of speech and literary expression. In other words, what Lenin was demanding was the unconditional 'party-mindedness' of journalists and writers who were Party members, not as an aesthetic rule but as a political one.

After brilliantly exposing the hypocrisy of the notion of 'absolute freedom' of writers and artists in the capitalist world, Lenin contrasts this 'hypocritically free' literature with 'a really free one that will be *openly* linked to the proletariat'. It is not a concrete demand but a dream of the future when, at the end of the article, he writes:

It will be a free literature, because the idea of socialism and sympathy with the working people, and not greed or careerism, will bring ever new forces to its ranks. It will be a free literature, because it will serve, not some satiated heroine, not the bored 'upper ten thousand' suffering from fatty degeneration, but the millions and tens of millions cf working people – the flower of the country, its strength and its future. It will be a free literature, enriching the last word in the revolutionary thought of mankind with the experience and living work of the socialist proletariat, bringing about permanent interaction between the experience of the past (scientific socialism, the completion of the development of socialism from its primitive, utopian forms) and the experience of the present (the present struggle of the worker comrades).[292]

In a letter written in May 1937, Nadezhda Krupskaya, the companion of Lenin's life and work, confirms our analysis of this often misused article. In this letter, which was published in the review *Druzhba Narodov*, No. IV, 1960, we read: 'It is always necessary to say on what occasion and in what context an article was written ... Lenin's articles *On Proletarian Culture, Party Organization and Party Literature*, and *The Tasks of the Young Communist League* do not apply to works of artistic literature.' We cannot doubt that Krupskaya was closer to Lenin and was better acquainted with his intentions than his latterday epigones.

Lenin was not infallible, nor did he ever, for a single moment, believe that he was. To present his saying and writings as Holy Writ is to deny the essential nature of Lenin the great revolutionary, always looking ahead, often mistaken, always willing to admit his errors.

His greatest work was the October Revolution; but even this work he recognized to be the complex product of subjective and objective factors. He said again and again that in the event of a socialist revolution being successful in an advanced country, Russia could no longer stand in the forefront of the forces of international revolution. The socialist revolution was the central problem of his life: all his thoughts, all his calculations began and ended with it. He was the greatest tactician and strategist in the history of the revolutionary working-class movement. But the 'dreamer in the Kremlin' never dreamed that, to celebrate the fiftieth anniversary of the revolution which he led to victory, a monument would be erected in the Kremlin which – artistic ineptitude apart – depicted him, not as the Prometheus of our century, but as an earnest, unimaginative bureaucrat.

NOTES

1. V. I. Lenin, *Collected Works*, Foreign Languages Publishing House, 1960, published in Great Britain by Lawrence & Wishart, Vol. 25, p. 492.
2. Vol. 1, pp. 159–60.
3. ibid., p. 194.
4. ibid., p. 236.
5. ibid., p. 298.
6. ibid., p. 328.
7. Vol. 4, p. 211.
8. ibid., p. 212.
9. Vol. 5, p. 373.
10. ibid., p. 375.
11. ibid., p. 392.
12. ibid., p. 416 (footnote).
13. ibid., p. 423.
14. ibid., p. 467.
15. ibid., pp. 509–10.
16. Vol. 11, p. 173.
17. ibid., p. 178.
18. Vol. 33, pp. 476–80.
19. Vol. 5, p. 508.
20. ibid., p. 355.
21. ibid., p. 480.
22. Vol. 7, p. 258.
23. ibid., p. 389.
24. ibid., p. 392.
25. ibid., pp. 396–7.
26. ibid., p. 415.
27. Vol. 31, p. 423.
28. Vol. 32, pp. 43–4.
29. *Marx in His Own Words*, Ernst Fischer and Franz Marek. Allen Lane The Penguin Press, London, 1970, pp. 130–1.
30. V. I. Lenin, *Collected Works*, Vol. 9, p. 29.
31. ibid., p. 44.
32. ibid., pp. 49–52.
33. ibid., p. 52.
34. ibid., p. 57.
35. ibid., p. 87.
36. ibid., p. 100.
37. ibid., p. 114.
38. ibid., p. 130.
39. ibid., p. 434.
40. Vol. 21, p. 33.
41. ibid., pp. 339–40.
42. ibid., p. 369.
43. ibid., p. 382.
44. ibid., p. 420.

45. Vol. 22, p. 197.
46. ibid., p. 205.
47. ibid., p. 241.
48. ibid., p. 262.
49. Vol. 21, p. 342.
50. Vol. 23, p. 79.
51. ibid., p. 297.
52. ibid., p. 299.
53. ibid , p. 307.
54. ibid., p. 350.
55. ibid., pp. 371–3.
56. Vol. 28, p. 33.
57. ibid., p. 37.
58. ibid., p. 75.
59. ibid., p. 78.
60. ibid., pp. 82–3.
61. ibid., p. 113.
62. ibid., p. 131.
63. ibid., pp. 476–7.
64. ibid., p. 485.
65. Vol. 29, p. 119.
66. ibid., p. 197.
67. ibid., p. 271.
68. ibid., p. 307.
69. ibid., p. 391.
70. ibid., p. 493.
71. Vol. 30, p. 208.
72. ibid., p. 308.
73. Vol. 20, p. 453.
74. Vol. 21, pp. 103–4.
75. Vol. 22, p. 310.
76. ibid., p. 312.
77. ibid., pp. 355–6.
78. Vol. 29, p. 253.
79. Vol. 36, pp. 605–10.
80. Vol. 30, pp. 160–1.
81. Vol. 31, p. 138.

82. ibid., p. 146.
83. Vol. 33, pp. 349–50.
84. ibid., pp. 499–500.
85. Vol. 31, p. 91.
86. ibid., p. 92.
87. ibid., p. 92.
88. Vol. 29, p. 387.
89. Vol. 32, p. 465.
90. ibid., p. 465.
91. ibid., p. 466.
92. Vol. 25, pp. 386, 424.
93. ibid., pp. 473–4.
94. Vol. 23, p. 321.
95. ibid., p. 328.
96. Vol. 25, p. 474.
97. ibid., p. 481.
98. ibid., p. 445.
99. Vol. 35, p. 269.
100. Vol. 26, pp. 103–4.
101. Vol. 30, p. 361.
102. Vol. 26, p. 68.
103. Vol. 25, p. 366.
104. ibid., p. 373.
105. Vol. 26, pp. 22–3.
106. ibid., p. 25.
107. ibid., pp. 67–8.
108. ibid., p. 83–4.
109. ibid., p. 119.
110. ibid., p. 130.
111. Vol. 36, p. 597
112. ibid., p. 596.
113. Vol. 23, p. 95.
114. Vol. 25, p. 412.
115. Vol. 27, pp. 264–5.
116. ibid., p. 268.
117. ibid., p. 273.
118. Vol. 28, p. 71.

119. ibid., p. 236.
120. ibid., pp. 247–8.
121. ibid., pp. 253–4.
122. ibid., p. 273.
123. ibid., p. 293.
124. ibid., p. 427.
125. ibid., p. 427.
126. Vol. 29, p. 109.
127. ibid., p. 183.
128. ibid., p. 373.
129. ibid., pp. 380–1.
130. ibid., pp. 388–9.
131. ibid., pp. 419–20.
132. ibid., p. 427.
133. Vol. 30, pp. 108–13.
134. Vol. 31, pp. 23–4.
135. ibid., pp. 44–5.
136. Vol. 32, p. 20.
137. ibid., p. 24.
138. ibid., pp. 56–7.
139. ibid., p. 68.
140. Vol. 33, p. 295.
141. Vol. 5, p. 425.
142. Vol. 9, p. 60.
143. Vol. 17, pp. 115–16.
144. Vol. 21, p. 339.
145. Vol. 22, pp. 344–5.
146. Vol. 23, p. 84.
147. ibid., pp. 158–9.
148. Vol. 25, p. 333.
149. ibid., p. 337.
150. ibid., p. 360.
151. ibid., p. 419.
152. ibid., pp. 452–3.
153. Vol. 31, p. 32.
154. ibid., p. 37.
155. ibid., pp. 37–8.
156. Vol. 25, p. 305.
157. Vol. 27, pp. 275–6.
158. ibid., pp. 276–7.
159. ibid., p. 19.
160. ibid., p. 29.
161. ibid., p. 36.
162. ibid., p. 39.
163. Vol. 30, pp. 491–2.
164. Vol. 31, pp. 24–5.
165. ibid., p. 28.
166. ibid., p. 47.
167. ibid., pp. 52–3.
168. ibid., p. 53.
169. ibid., p. 54.
170. ibid., p. 56.
171. ibid., p. 58.
172. ibid., p. 268.
173. ibid., p. 66.
174. ibid., pp. 67–8.
175. ibid., p. 70.
176. ibid., p. 74.
177. ibid., pp. 84–5.
178. ibid., pp. 92–3.
179. ibid., pp. 403–4.
180. ibid., pp. 114–15.
181. Vol. 32, p. 468.
182. ibid., p. 476.
183. Vol. 31, p. 51.
184. ibid., pp. 96–7.
185. ibid., p. 91.
186. Vol. 25, p. 281.
187. Vol. 27, p. 274.
188. Vol. 31, pp. 35–6 (footnote).
189. ibid., p. 36.
190. Vol. 13, pp. 18–9.
191. ibid., pp. 22–3.

192. ibid., p. 26.
193. ibid., p. 33.
194. ibid., p. 34.
195. ibid., p. 36.
196. ibid., pp. 39–40.
197. ibid., p. 48.
198. Vol. 25, p. 183.
199. ibid., p. 184.
200. ibid., p. 185.
201. ibid., p. 186.
202. ibid., pp. 189–90.
203. Vol. 33, pp. 204–5.
204. Vol. 29, p. 342.
205. Vol. 31, p. 64.
206. Vol. 21, p. 420.
207. Vol. 27, p. 238.
208. ibid., p. 245.
209. ibid., p. 246.
210. ibid., p. 247.
211. ibid., p. 249.
212. ibid., pp. 261–3.
213. ibid., p. 337.
214. Vol. 28, pp. 426–7.
215. Vol. 32, pp. 20–1.
216. ibid., pp. 61–2.
217. ibid., pp. 97–8.
218. ibid., pp. 186–8.
219. ibid., pp. 215–18.
220. ibid., pp. 316–18.
221. ibid., pp. 342–3.
222. ibid., p. 365.
223. ibid., p. 459.
224. ibid., pp. 480–1.
225. Vol. 33, pp. 23–4.
226. ibid., pp. 58–9.
227. ibid., pp. 271–2.
228. ibid., pp. 273–4.

229. ibid., pp. 275–6.
230. ibid., p. 304.
231. ibid., p. 468.
232. ibid., pp. 469–70.
233. ibid., p. 474.
234. ibid., p. 501.
235. Vol. 29, p. 183.
236. Vol. 22, pp. 275–6.
237. ibid., p. 295.
238. ibid., p. 312.
239. Vol. 21, pp. 15–16.
240. ibid., p. 18.
241. ibid., p. 34.
242. ibid., p. 242.
243. ibid., p. 299.
244. ibid., p. 300.
245. ibid., pp. 328–9.
246. Vol. 23, pp. 32–3.
247. ibid., p. 268.
248. Vol. 26, pp. 311–12.
249. ibid., pp. 349–50.
250. ibid., pp. 448–9.
251. Vol. 27, p. 46.
252. ibid., pp. 59–60.
253. ibid., p. 69.
254. ibid., pp. 71–2.
255. ibid., pp. 162–3.
256. ibid., pp. 292–3.
257. Vol. 30, pp. 50–1.
258. ibid., p. 191.
259. ibid., pp. 318–20.
260. ibid., pp. 365–7.
261. ibid., p. 453.
262. ibid., p. 487.
263. Vol. 31, p. 412.
264. ibid., p. 475.
265. Vol. 33, p. 213.

266. ibid., p. 217.
267. ibid., p. 357.
268. ibid., p. 447.
269. ibid., p. 500.
270. Vol. 23, p. 250.
271. Vol. 37, p. 426.
272. Vol. 14, p. 46.
273. ibid., p. 69.
274. ibid., p. 123.
275. ibid., p. 130.
276. ibid., p. 137.
277. ibid., p. 262.
278. ibid., p. 326.
279. ibid., p. 358.

280. Vol. 38, p. 98.
281. ibid., pp. 167–8.
282. ibid., p. 180.
283. ibid., p. 182.
284. ibid., p. 194.
285. ibid., p. 276.
286. ibid., p. 278.
287. ibid., p. 363.
288. Vol. 10, pp. 44–5.
289. ibid., p. 45.
290. ibid., pp. 45–6.
291. ibid., pp. 47–8.
292. ibid., pp. 48–9.

INDEX